DATE DUE

A Note from the Editor

You are about to take a journey backward in time. Your means of transportation will be the written word and some glorious photographs. Your journey will take you, decade by decade, through the 20th century . . . our century.

Many of the events described in each issue of *Our Century* magazine are famous. Some have perhaps been forgotten. Many of the people were extraordinary, some merely ordinary, a few certainly evil. But all these events and people have one thing in common: they have made this century a fascinating and momentous one.

All of us who worked on *Our Century* hope you find your journey into the past interesting and educational. And most of all we hope you enjoy these "snapshots in time" as much as we enjoyed recapturing them for you.

Tony Napolo
Editor-in-Chief, *Our Century*

Statistics

	1920	1930
Population of the United States	105.7 million	123.1 million
Number of states in the United States	48	48
Population by race:		
White	94.8 million	110.3 million
Negro	10.4 million	11.9 million
Other	426,574	878,078
Population by sex:		
Male	53.9 million	62.2 million
Female	51.8 million	60.9 million
Population per square mile	35.5	41.2
Life expectancy in years:		
White male	56.3	59.1
White female	58.5	62.7
Negro male	47.1	46.9
Negro female	47.6	49.5
Deaths per 100,000 persons:		
From measles	8.8	3.2
From motor vehicle accidents	10.3	26.7
Number of homicides	5,815	10,331
Number of lynchings	61	21
Number of horses	19.7 million	13.5 million
Number of bowlers	27,000	219,000
Unemployment rate	4.0%	8.7%
Average hourly wage (unskilled male)	53¢	48¢
Number of dentists	33,000	62,000
Number of authors	35,000	57,000
Number of paperboys	28,000	39,000
Number of students graduating from high school	311,000	667,000
Passenger cars sold	1,905,500	2,787,400
Number of daily newspapers	2,042	1,942
Number of AM radio stations	1	618
Prices:		
dozen eggs	68¢	44¢
quart of milk	17¢	14¢
loaf of bread	12¢	9¢
pound of butter	70¢	46¢
pound of bacon	52¢	42¢
pound of round steak	42¢	42¢
pound of coffee	47¢	39¢

OUR CENTURY

For a free color catalog describing Gareth Stevens's list of high-quality children's books, call 1-800-341-3569 (USA) or 1-800-461-9120 (Canada).

ISBN 0-8368-1034-1

This North American edition published by
Gareth Stevens Publishing
1555 North RiverCenter Drive, Suite 201
Milwaukee, Wisconsin 53212, USA

This edition first published in 1993 by Gareth Stevens, Inc. Originally published in 1989 by Fearon Education, 500 Harbor Boulevard, Belmont, California, 94002, with © 1989 by Fearon Education. End matter © 1993 by Gareth Stevens, Inc.

Printed in the United States of America

1 2 3 4 5 6 7 8 9 98 97 96 95 94 93

All photographs: The Bettmann Archive, with the following exceptions: pp. 5, 7: National Archives; pp. 23, 29, 45, 50: UPI/Bettmann Newsphotos. Advertisements on endpapers: The D'Arcy Collection, University of Illinois at Urbana-Champaign.

1920–1930

Gareth Stevens Publishing
MILWAUKEE

Instant News On Elections

Radio Enters America's Homes

Everyone in the family leaned forward, listening carefully. It was November 2, 1920. The election results were just coming in.

They heard the results clearly. Harding had won by a landslide.

It was hard to believe! Not that Harding had won—they knew all along that he'd whip Cox. It was hard to believe they'd heard it in their own home. The broadcast had come from station KDKA in Pittsburgh.

Americans had just heard the first scheduled, public radio program. There had been tests and experiments before. But this was an actual news broadcast. Maybe radio was more than a toy after all.

Soon there'd be much more to hear on this wonderful new device.

Only a few hundred people heard that first broadcast. KDKA was the only public radio station in 1920. But a year and a half later there were 220 stations in America.

At first there were a number of names for the new invention. Some called it "wireless telephone" or "wireless music box." Another term was "radio telephone." Eventually, people settled for simply "radio."

The first radios cost from $50 to $150. By 1922 they were in some 3,000,000 homes across the country.

America was showing its interest by spending its money. In 1922 Americans spent $60 million on radios and equipment. The next year they spent $136 million!

In 1925 some 50 million people were listening to radio. And they heard more than election returns. Music took up over 60% of the broadcast time. But there were also lectures, children's stories, and news reports.

At first there weren't many drama programs. But sporting events quickly became popular. In 1921 a championship boxing match was broadcast. Listeners heard a blow by blow report of the Dempsey-Carpentier fight.

Live World Series Broadcast

The announcer wasn't actually at the fight. There was no equipment yet to broadcast from outside the station. So how did they do it? Someone at ringside telephoned the match to the announcer in the studio. He

then repeated it over the radio. Live or not, it was convincing to the radio audience.

By the next year, though, portable equipment had been developed. The 1922 World Series between the Yankees and Giants was broadcast live.

Radio was also used for serious purposes. In 1921 Herbert Hoover asked Americans to help war-torn Europe. He used the radio to get his message across.

By the middle of the 1920s, radio was worrying newspaper owners. People didn't have to wait for the paper to find out the news. They could hear about events as soon as they happened.

But most people listened to the radio for entertainment. As early as 1923 listeners enjoyed variety shows. The first was *The Eveready Hour,* from station WEAF. It featured songs, comedy, and dramatic skits. It also presented famous movie, vaudeville, and stage performers.

By the end of 1925 there were several weekly comedy programs. *The Smith Family* was very popular. Later, this show was called *Fibber*

McGee and Molly. The Happiness Boys and *The Gold Dust Twins* were also popular shows.

The first paid commercial was aired in 1922. A builder paid station WEAF $100 to talk about his projects. From then on, radio had a way to make money.

For a long time advertisers didn't try to "hard sell" products. Many just made sure their name was part of the program's name. The *Eveready Hour* was sponsored by Eveready Battery Company. The *Ipana Troubadors* was sponsored by Ipana Toothpaste.

In the earliest years of radio there were many problems. For example, different stations tried to broadcast on the same radio frequency. Finally, in 1927, the Radio Law was passed. It set up a govern-ment agency to handle such problems.

At first, radio stations could only broadcast a short distance. But by 1925, President Coolidge's inaugural speech was heard across the nation. No one station was powerful enough to send it that far. It went through a chain, each station passing it on to the next.

The idea for networks came next. Soon NBC and CBS had their own station chains. Many smaller stations couldn't afford to have famous performers. With networks, though, the best performers could be heard everywhere.

By 1929 radio was big business. That year, Americans spent $852 million on radios and equipment. Every third home in the country had one. The "Radio Age" had arrived. ∎

By 1925 millions of American families like this one often gathered together for an evening of radio listening.

Immigration Quotas Passed

America's Gateway Starts to Close

Ellis Island covers only a dozen or so acres of land. That isn't much, compared to the rest of the United States. But for millions of Americans, it is the land they will never forget. To them it is the Gateway to Freedom.

From 1607 to 1920 people flocked to America. They came from around the world. Their reasons for leaving their old countries were many. But they had one thing in common. They all hoped to find a better life in America.

Until 1855 there were no restrictions on immigrants. America was a big country—land of wide open spaces. The more people who came, the more prosperous the country would become.

By the mid-1800s though, trouble was in the air. Many Americans took a dislike to foreigners. Much of their feeling was based on fear. They feared immigrants would steal their jobs. And they were afraid of the newcomers' religions and political beliefs.

Because of those fears, new immigration laws went into effect in 1855. From then on, immigrants had to pass an inspection to stay here.

An Immigration Commission was formed. It was located in New York City. The Commission could bar immigrants who had diseases or criminal records. It could also keep out people because of their political views.

Eventually the Immigration Commission moved to Ellis Island, about a mile southwest of New York City.

Over the years it has been the gateway for a huge number of immigrants. The first of them arrived at Ellis Island in 1892. Between then and 1920, almost 17 million more arrived. In 1907 alone, more than 1.2 million people landed there.

Once the immigrants arrived they underwent a "screening" process. For many, the process was frightening. First the new arrivals were taken from their ships to the island. Then they were led to a huge building. There they had to leave their bags on the ground floor.

That in itself was often frightening. Many people had everything they owned in their bags. How could they be sure their things wouldn't be lost or stolen?

On the second floor the newcomers took a medical examination. If they had infectious diseases they were sent to detention centers. The centers were fenced with wire. To many they must have seemed like jails.

There were medical clinics in the detention centers. Sick immigrants had to stay there until they were cured. Then they could continue on. About 2% were thought to be incurable. These people were sent back to their native country.

After passing the medical exams, they were questioned by legal inspectors. They were asked about 30 questions. What is your name? Where were you born? Do you have a job waiting for you in America? They were also asked if they were criminals or anarchists.

If the inspectors didn't like the answers, the immigrants underwent more questioning.

Immigrants who passed all the tests were given landing cards. They could go to the mainland. They were free. Their life in America was about to begin.

The first big reduction in immigration came in 1914. Then the Great War in Europe cut into the number of people migrating to America.

In 1917 a literacy law was passed. That meant that immigrants had to know how to read before they entered America. The law was supposed to ensure that immigrants would be useful to America. President Wilson refused to sign it. He said it was unfair to poor people. In many countries they never had a chance to learn to read. But feelings against foreigners were growing stronger. Congress passed the law over his veto.

When America entered the war in 1917, Ellis Island was given a new role. The Army and Navy took it over. It was used as a hospital for emergency treatment.

The "Red Scare"

In the summer of 1919, the Immigration Service took over the island again. Because of a new law, the role of Ellis Island changed once more. During the war, there had been a great fear of German spies. After the war there was a "Red Scare."

The Communist Revolution in Russia frightened many Americans. They thought the Reds might take over the United States. Because of that fear, the new law was passed. It made it easier to deport anarchists or anyone who wanted to overthrow the government by force or violence.

Ellis Island was used to hold undesirable people. They stayed there until the paper work to get rid of them was completed. Then they were deported from America.

In 1921 the Emergency Act was signed by President Harding. This law set up a quota system for immigrants. It was heavily in favor of immigrants from northern and western Europe. It was meant to limit the number of Jewish and Italian immigrants. Sup-

posedly, it would also keep Communists out of the country.

In 1924 a stricter law was passed. Even fewer immigrants from southern and eastern Europe were allowed. And the National Origins Act of 1929 was more restrictive than any before. It limited total immigration to 150,000 people a year. Like earlier laws, it favored northern and western Europeans.

No Africans at all were permitted to migrate to America. But the law didn't affect people from the western

hemisphere. Immigration from Canada, Mexico, and the West Indies actually increased.

By the end of the 1920s the effect of the quota laws was easy to see. Ellis Island seemed like a ghost town. On just one day in 1907, about 11,000 people waited to be processed on Ellis Island. The total number of immigrants for *all* of 1929 was only 35,000.

It looked like fear had done its work. It looked like the gateway to freedom would soon be closed. ∎

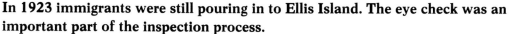

In 1923 immigrants were still pouring in to Ellis Island. The eye check was an important part of the inspection process.

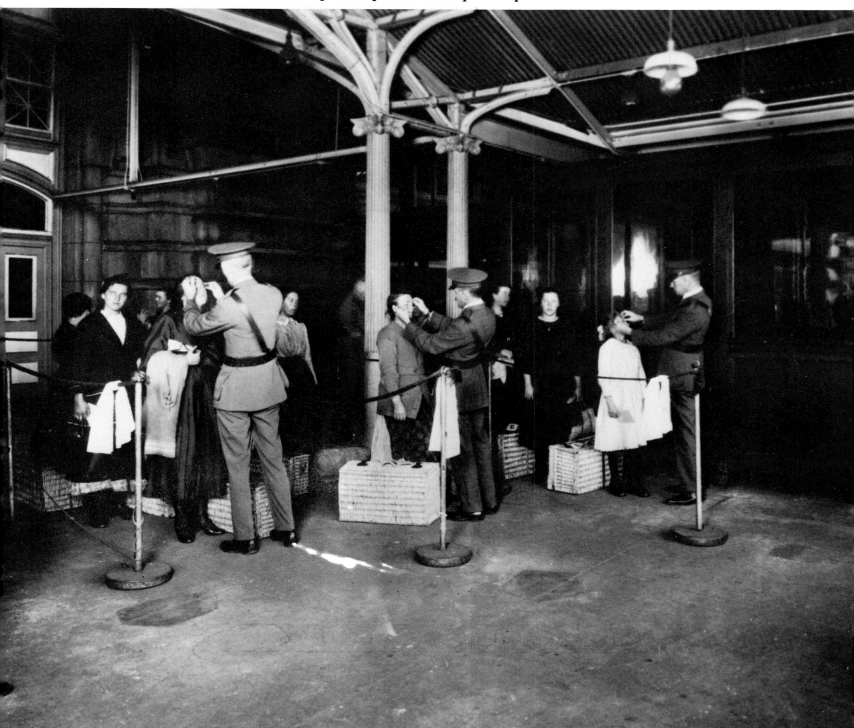

Freedom Is Key to Fashion

Skirts and Stocks Go Up and Down

Plaid puttees hide the actress's legs but add a dash of fun. Before the decade is out silk stockings will replace the puttees. But the fur coat stayed in style throughout the '20s.

"Freedom" has been the overall fashion theme of the '20s. The most recognizable single style belonged to the "Flapper." She was the "new woman of the decade." Freedom was at the heart of her life.

The Great War had given women more independence. And they didn't want to give it up when the war ended. As they asserted their newfound freedom, skirt and hemlines rose.

In 1920 that trend shocked a writer for the *New York Times*. To him, the new styles were indecent. He wrote, "The American woman has lifted her skirts far beyond any modest limitation."

The hem length was 9 inches from the ground. The next year skirts rose higher! One man said that skirt lengths were like the stock market. And in a way, that was true. They started low, dipped a few times, and then soared. By the end of 1929, both dropped fast.

Before the war, women's clothing had been heavy and awkward. By 1928, light, comfortable clothing was the style. And as skirts got short, women started wearing silk or rayon stockings. They also changed from cotton to silk or rayon underwear.

The *Journal of Commerce* reported the difference. In 1913 the average woman's costume used some 19 yards of cloth. By 1928 only 7 yards were needed.

Girls called "Flappers" wore thin dresses with short sleeves. For evening wear, they might have no sleeves at all. They rolled down the tops of the stocking as a daring stunt. The kneecap was exposed for all to see!

In 1921 some lawmakers in Utah wanted to ban the new styles. They thought skirts should be no higher than three inches from the ground. They wanted to fine flappers who wore shorter skirts. They even wanted to put them in jail! In Virginia lawmakers tried to outlaw low-cut gowns. Showing three inches of a woman's throat was enough, they said. But despite the lawmakers, the styles went right on changing.

Suzanne Lenglen helped make the newer styles popular. She is a champion tennis player. Her picture appeared in newspapers around the world. In 1922 at Wimbledon, England, her clothing stunned the crowd and newspaper readers. She didn't wear the usual, ankle-length tennis costume. Her dress ended just below her knees!

It was shocking to a lot of people. But it helped her play the game better. She also wore a headband to keep her hair out of her eyes. That too became a fashion.

Short hair for women was another style trend of the '20s. Some women first wore their hair short while doing war work. That may have been how the fashion started. But by 1925 it was the style everywhere. At first, short hair was considered daring. In 1920 F. Scott Fitzgerald wrote a short story "Bernice Bobs Her Hair." It appeared in his book, *Flappers and Philosophers*. The story showed how a new hair style could upset society.

Movies played a big role in American life during this decade. What the stars did, their admirers imitated. Once Clara Bow cut off her long curls, what girl would want long hair? The popular cloche hat added to the new look. It didn't look right on women with long hair. The hat and the short hairstyle made a perfect fit.

The widespread use of makeup also made news. Lipstick, rouge, and eye shadow used to be only for "bad" girls. In the '20s, though, "beauty" became a business. It was no longer something women tried to hide.

"Oxford Bags" were all the rage in trousers. This fellow, though, may have pushed the style past its limits.

In 1919 the *Ladies' Home Journal* carried an ad for rouge. It said that nobody would notice the makeup "if properly applied." Just ten years later the magazine carried another ad for rouge. This time the message was different. It boasted that the scarlet makeup "will stay with you for hours."

Young men in the '20s had their own fashion statements to make. They broke away from the stuffy business clothes of their elders. Some items were designed more for shock value than for comfort.

As an example, consider the wide-legged pants called "Oxford Bags." They were often bigger around in the legs than in the waist. If it rained, the pants soaked up a lot of water. In wet weather, men had to hold them up with both hands. A pinched-waist jacket made a good match for the "bags." For those who could afford it, a raccoon coat added even more class. And a broad-brimmed hat often topped off the outfit.

As 1929 ended, baggy pants were gone and skirt lengths were dropping. Longer hair was coming back in style. Evening gowns swept the ground. Long white gloves covered the once-bare arms.

The fun of the '20s was giving way to more serious things. The "jazz babies" were growing up. ∎

The Flapper
Jazz Baby of the '20s

With her cloche hat, low-belted dress, and her knees almost showing, this 1925 Flapper is dressed in high style. Her silk stockings and patent-leather high-heels draw attention to her legs. This is just what the old folks were afraid of.

Her hair was short, and so was her skirt. She liked to dance, but Marathon dancing didn't suit her. The Charleston was her kind of dance—lively and full of fun. They called her a *flapper*.

Like so much else in the '20s, she was a product of the Great War. American women started to find more freedom during the war years. Many worked at jobs that supported our soldiers. In Red Cross work or entertaining troops, they began to travel.

In 1920 the new freedom was even shown in a new law. For the first time women were allowed to vote. The times were indeed changing. The idea of the helpless little woman was fading away.

The flapper's music, of course, was jazz. It stood for what *she* stood for—freedom, fun, and forget the future. Live for today—that's the thing.

In the eyes of many, she was a *bad* girl. She put on her lipstick in public—and even smoked cigarettes! Out of the public eye, she might even drink bootleg liquor. And, it was said, she was crazy about kissing.

"I've kissed a dozen men. I suppose I'll kiss a dozen more." So said a bold young lady in F. Scott Fitzgerald's hit book, *This Side of Paradise*. In 1920 that was shocking. Not only did these fresh young girls kiss—they bragged about it!

That same year Fitzgerald came out with another novel, *Flappers and Philosophers*. In it, he told more about the "new woman."

But it wasn't until 1925 that flappers really came into their own. That was just about the time a dance called the Charleston became popular in America. But the style of the flapper didn't stay at home. In Europe, too, hems went up and young women stepped out.

By the end of the 1920s the flapper was gone. She had kicked up a fuss and had her fun. After the crash on Wall Street, though, the party ended.

But while it lasted it had been some party. And the flapper had been at center stage, dancing her cares away. ■

Civil War in Russia Ends

The Great War had been over for more than a year. It was 1920 and the nations of western Europe were learning to live peacefully.

In Russia, though, fighting raged on. The Bolshevik Party had overthrown the Russian government in 1917. Now they were in their third year of running the country. Vladimir Lenin was the leader of the Bolsheviks (they changed their name to Communists in 1918) and the head of the Russian government.

The Bolsheviks had signed a treaty with Germany during the Great War. Lenin knew the treaty was unfair to Russia. He had signed it only because he had little choice. Russia was in desperate need of food, and the government had no money. There simply were no resources to go on fighting.

After overthrowing the Russian government, the Bolsheviks found they had much opposition to their rule. Some Russians were against them because they had made peace with Germany. Others were against the idea of a "socialist" government. Lenin's party planned to remove all private ownership of land, property, and businesses. They wanted to put them under control of the "state." As time went on the opposition to the Communists grew. Finally full civil war erupted in 1918.

The Red Army was led by Leon Trotsky. It was fighting for the defense of the Communist state. The collection of armies that combined to oppose them was called the White Army. Several generals who had fought under the Russian Tsar were in control of various White Army regiments.

Opposition to the Communists also came from outside Russia. Forces from Europe, Japan, and the United States entered the conflict against the Red Army. Each country had its own reasons for becoming involved.

Allies Help Fight the Reds

In the spring of 1918, Japanese troops landed at Vladivostok in far eastern Russia. In the summer, British and American troops arrived. These countries claimed they ⇨

American troops march past their headquarters in Vladivostok in 1919. They would remain in control of the city for another year.

were protecting their property. During the Great War they had stored ammunition at Vladivostok. At that time it was kept there to help the Russians fight the Germans. Then the Bolsheviks had signed the treaty with Germany. The Allies said they wanted to keep Germany from getting the ammunition.

But there were other reasons as well. Many of these other nations feared the Communists. They were afraid that a Communist revolution might spread to their own countries.

So the Allies did more than just protect their ammunition. They also gave armed support to the White Army. Their goal was to help defeat the Communists.

Despite Allied help, the White Army faced a major problem. It lacked support from the people in the country. Basically, the White Army wanted to bring back the tsar. The people didn't. Most of them preferred the Communists to the tsar. Also, the White Army treated the people badly. Its soldiers were as cruel as the tsar's troops had been.

No Support Among the People

There was a common thread that ran through all the separate armies that made up the White Army. A general or an admiral would set up his own government out in the Russian provinces. Then he'd get support from Allied forces. Next he would attack the Communists in one of their two strong bases of power, Moscow or Petrograd. At first the general or admiral would have the support of the peasants. But then word would spread that he wanted to bring back the tsar. He'd lose the support of the people. Then the Red Army would attack and defeat his forces.

In 1920 the Communists took back control of Vladivostok. Their victory in the civil war was almost completed.

This pattern occurred all over Russia. It happened with Admiral Kolchak and his forces in Siberia, and with Admiral Wrangel and his troops in the Crimea. And it was also what happened with General Deniken, commander of the Cossacks.

The Red Army was most concerned with the fighting around Moscow. That city was the heart of the country. And since 1918 it had been the nation's capital. By 1920, though, Moscow was safe from the White Army. The Red Army was able to wipe out any remaining pockets of resistance.

Why had the White Army lost power? The Europeans were tired of war. There was little support at home for pushing into Russia. The Allies had been at war for years. Their people wanted an end to the fighting. They decided that the Communists posed no direct threat to their countries.

The American forces had planned to hold Vladivostok while the White Army moved west and took Moscow. But that never happened. By early 1920, the White Army regiments in the region had lost the people's support and the Red Army recaptured Vladivostok.

As more towns in Siberia began to fall, the Allies decided to pull out. The Americans were in an awkward position. All they wanted to do was get out of Russia. But the Red Army was blocking their way. Then one fortunate event saved them. Some months before, they had captured a large supply of gold. When they agreed to leave it behind, they were allowed to leave peacefully.

By the end of 1920, the Red Army had done its job. In the east, it had defeated its enemies in Siberia. It had driven the Poles out of the west. And it had taken control of the Crimea in the south.

Led by Lenin and Trotsky, the Reds had defeated all their enemies. Finally, Russia was completely under Communist control. ■

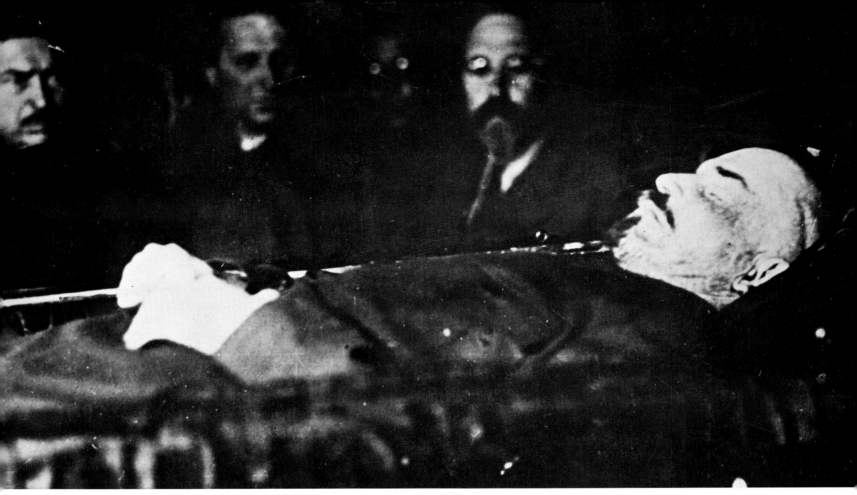

Vladimir Lenin, the leader of the world's first communist nation, lies in state in Moscow's Red Square.

Lenin Dead at 53

Stalin, Trotsky Vie For Control

The nation mourned. He had led them through the Revolution. He had led them through the Civil War. Now, Vladimir Ilich Lenin, the father of the Soviet Union, was dead.

For several years he had been in bad health. In 1918 he had been shot twice by a political enemy. At that time, he said there was no real harm done. But his health weakened over the years.

He continued to push himself. He worked long hours and rarely rested. In the spring of 1922 he suffered a paralyzing stroke. Doctors said it was a result of the gunshot wounds. In the next year, Lenin suffered two more strokes. Finally, on January 21, 1924, he died.

Lenin's body lay in state for a week. Hundreds of thousands of Soviet citizens came to see it. Even-

tually, the body was embalmed and put in a glass coffin. Today it rests on permanent display in Moscow's Red Square.

Lenin had ruled the country since the Revolution of 1917. In those seven years, he hadn't picked a successor. At the time of his death the leadership of the Soviet Union was open. Two men looked promising for the job. Both were close to Lenin and held important government jobs.

One of the men was Leon Trotsky, founder of the Red Army. He had worked with Lenin since before the Revolution. He felt that he should succeed Lenin as leader of the Communist party and the Soviet Union. His goal was to spread communism around the world.

Another candidate for the top job was Josef Stalin. He too had ⇨

worked with Lenin before the Revolution. He disagreed with Trotsky on the importance of spreading communism to other countries. First he wanted to build "socialism in one country."

Before he died, Lenin had warned the party about Stalin. Lenin said that Stalin didn't have the proper qualities to be a good leader. Basically, he said that Stalin was too crude, too lacking in judgment.

Stalin may have been crude, but he was also crafty. For some time, he had been putting his friends in high places. Their support helped when the showdown came between him and Trotsky.

After winning the power struggle with Leon Trotsky, Josef Stalin succeeded Lenin as leader of the Soviet Union.

In the fight for power, Trotsky brought up Lenin's warnings about Stalin. Stalin's supporters defended him. They said that he had admitted to his faults. He was willing to change.

Then they pointed out that Trotsky had opposed Lenin in the past. This charge was also true. At one time, before the revolution, Trotsky had not supported Lenin's Bolshevik party.

Stalin in Control

Little by little, Stalin was able to take more power. By 1929 he was in complete control. Trotsky had been disgraced and forced to leave the country.

Stalin had a big job ahead of him. The Soviet Union needed to be brought up to the standards of Western countries. To accomplish this, Stalin wanted to make the country more dependent on industry rather than on farming. He declared that the change would be done through a "five-year plan." To Stalin, modernization was like a military goal. The end result was the important thing. Those opposed to it would be overcome with force.

During the Civil War, Lenin had called for "war communism." The government had taken strict control of business. In 1923 Lenin began the New Economic Policy (NEP). That permitted some private businesses to operate. Farmers were allowed to sell extra food and keep the profits.

By the end of the decade, the NEP had been discontinued. Nothing would be allowed to interfere with modernization. Private farms would no longer be permitted. All farms would become government farms. The *kulaks*, owners of profitable farms, were now considered enemies. They would be treated harshly. Nothing must stand in the way of the Five-Year Plan.

Josef Stalin's real name was Josef Djugashvili. He had taken the name Stalin when he was fighting the tsar. It is well chosen. The name means "man of steel." ∎

Benito Mussolini (center, suit and tie) led thousands of his Fascist supporters in a march on Rome in October 1922.

Led By Mussolini

Thousands of Fascists March on Rome

As a young man, Benito Mussolini had been a Socialist. But in 1915 he left the party because the Socialists were against Italy entering the Great War. Mussolini felt that Italy should fight with the Allies against Germany. If the Italians joined their cause the Allies promised they would be rewarded with new lands after the war.

When Italy did enter the war,

Mussolini joined the army and was wounded. After the war he edited a newspaper in Milan. And he also became active in politics.

Mussolini was an angry man. Italy hadn't received the rewards it had been promised. He was angry with his country's political parties. He thought the Socialists were useless. And he didn't like the Communists at all. They seemed much more

interested in Russia than Italy. Mussolini didn't favor democracy, either.

Italy had a king and a parliament. But Mussolini didn't think that kind of rule worked. He felt Italy needed a strong national government like the great Caesars had in ancient Rome. With that kind of leadership, Italy could once again take its place in the world as a proud nation. ⇨

Mussolini brought together other men who were opposed to the Socialists and the Communists. At first this group called themselves Blackshirts. The name came from the military style outfits they wore. Later, they called themselves *Fascists*. This name came from the Italian word *fasci*. That means a bundle of rods tied together for strength. In ancient Rome, the men who enforced the laws carried *fasci* as weapons.

Like much of Europe after the war, Italy faced many problems. There weren't enough jobs. The economy was weak. Because of the people's unhappiness, the Communists began to gain strength.

Like all political parties, the Fascists needed money. People's fear of the Communists helped them get it. The Communists said they would put the workers in power. Owners of big businesses and other wealthy Italians didn't like that idea. So they gave money to Mussolini's party.

The Fascists had their headquarters in Milan. But Mussolini's heart was in Rome. He planned to use the capital city as his base of power. That was part of his plan to change the country. He dreamed that Rome would again become as powerful as it was in ancient times. And like Caesars of old, Mussolini would rule a great nation.

. . . Like Caesars of old, Mussolini would rule a great nation.

In October of 1922 Mussolini decided it was time to take action. Why wait to be voted in? Italy's government was in Rome. Mussolini sent word to all the Fascists in Italy to meet there. They were to go by car, train, plane, or on foot.

People in the government were worried. Would there be fighting in the streets? Would the Fascists start

a revolution? Prime Minister Luigi Facta wanted to stop the march. He thought the army should be called out to face the Fascists. But King Victor Emmanuel said no. He felt that would cause even more problems. In protest against the king's decision, Facta resigned.

Now the king didn't know what to do. Finally, he decided to appoint Mussolini prime minister. After all, Mussolini and his Fascists believed in a strong government. They wouldn't let the Communists cause trouble.

When the news spread across Italy, more and more people headed for Rome. Some had been afraid of the army. Now they had nothing to worry about.

On October 30, 1922, Mussolini triumphantly arrived in Rome. There was a huge parade. About 25,000 people supporting Mussolini and his Fascists marched through the streets. The "March on Rome" had succeeded! ∎

Opposition Outlawed

Il Duce Takes Charge

Once he became prime minister, Mussolini went into action. Quickly he began to seek full control of Italy. He told the king and parliament that he needed special powers. Italy was in trouble, he told them. People couldn't find jobs. Many who had jobs were on strike.

Mussolini claimed the Communists were causing most of the problems. He warned the government that if something wasn't done soon, more workers would join them. There would be more strikes. There might even be a revolution like the

one in Russia. Mussolini said he had a big job to do. And he had to do it fast.

Parliament agreed to Mussolini's demands. He was given almost total power. He became *Il Duce*—the leader and dictator.

Mussolini liked to refer to the days of ancient Rome. Then dictators were appointed in times of crisis. It was always just for a short time, until the crisis was past.

The Fascists had a little more than a year until the next elections were to be held. They used that time to secure their hold on the govern-

ment. They put their own men in government jobs. They worked out ways to change the election rules. They bribed some people into going along with them. Others, they bullied. Violence was a big part of the Fascist system.

Mussolini did not forget the wealthy men who had backed him. He cut taxes for big business. He gave big tax breaks to landlords. And he gave the banks large amounts of money.

But he also made conditions better for working people. He called for an 8-hour workday and a 40-hour workweek. By having the government set working conditions, he got rid of the unions. Strikes were no longer a threat.

Mussolini also made jobs for people in public works projects. Harbors were cleared. Bridges were built. He got things done. So long as there was no opposition, he could act quickly. Usually Mussolini himself was on hand when a new project began. He knew the value of publicity. And he was an excellent public speaker.

Fascists in Complete Control

In the 1924 elections, the Fascists won a huge victory. Their control of the election process wasn't the only reason. Many Italians were glad to make a trade-off. They gave up some of their freedom for security. If they had good working conditions, who needed a union? If the Fascists were doing a good job, who needed another party? With so much support behind him, Mussolini found it easy to get rid of all opposition.

Without opposition, Mussolini and the Fascists lost no time debating government policy. In this way it was easier to move the country ahead. One of Mussolini's goals was to make the trains run on time. To him, that was a symbol of a well-run country.

There were other needs, of course. The Communists had to be wiped out. Italy needed the land the Allies had promised. The country needed to stand out among nations. The only way to meet those goals was for the Fascists to rule without opposition.

Mussolini took more and more power upon himself. His enemies were beaten, jailed, or driven out of the country. Some were even murdered. The press came completely under his control. Eventually, even Parliament was abolished.

By 1928 *Il Duce* had total power. He and his Fascists have wiped out democracy and free speech in Italy. But the trains run on time. ∎

By the end of the decade, Mussolini had wiped out all his opponents and taken full control of the Italian government.

The Weimar Republic

Democracy Comes to Germany

When the Great War ended in 1918, the victorious Allies set the terms of the peace. One of the demands they made was that Germany's Kaiser Wilhelm give up his throne.

Rather than agree to do that, Wilhelm just left the country. But that wasn't enough for the Allies. They demanded that he must *never* come back. Otherwise, Germany would be made to suffer harsh penalties in return for peace.

The Kaiser's supporters found a solution. They simply announced that the Kaiser had quit. Then they turned the government over to the Social Democrats. Now the question was, what kind of government would Germany have? A monarchy was out of the question. The Allies already said they wouldn't permit the Germans to have a king.

The Communists in Germany were eager to have a government like the Soviet Union's. But too many Germans were opposed to the Reds. A Communist government would cause serious problems for business owners and the wealthy classes. Military men wanted the army to rule.

But the Allies would not allow that, either.

Phillip Scheidemann, a Social Democrat, came up with a solution. On November 9, 1918, all of Berlin awaited to hear what it was. A crowd stood in the streets outside the government building. Scheidemann went to the window and made an announcement. Germany, he said, was now a Democratic Republic. Almost by accident, democracy had come to Germany.

Military men wanted the army to rule.

In February 1919 the national assembly met in Weimar. Friedrich Ebert was elected president of Germany's first democracy. For better or worse, the Weimar Republic was in business. Many would say for worse.

Under the new democracy, political groups fought all the time. On the

left were the Communists who wanted to join the Soviet Union. On the right were the well-armed Free Corps. Its members hated democracy and thought of themselves as the nation's police.

The German economy grew more and more troubled. Many of the problems stemmed from the peace treaty. It had stripped Germany of territories it had once ruled. Some of that land was rich in iron ore, some in coal. The treaty also made Germany pay huge financial damages to its wartime enemies. U.S. president Woodrow Wilson had fought against making Germany pay such large amounts. He felt that it was better to get the country healthy again. If the German people were doing well, they'd be less likely to go to war again. But the other Allies felt differently.

In 1923 Germany could no longer pay its war debts to France. So the French took over the Ruhr, the industrial center of Germany. There were mines and factories there. Many Germans were put out of work. Riots and demonstrations followed. Finally, France withdrew.

It was a hard time for Germans. Their money had lost its value. Every day it was worth less. A man might get paid for a day's work. The next day that amount of money wouldn't buy a postage stamp. Everybody's savings were wiped out. People couldn't buy food. Finally, the Allies realized that Germany's problems could spread. At last, they stepped in to help.

The next year, Germany began to grow more stable. By 1926 the Weimar Republic was on its feet. The country was no longer an outcast among nations. German artists and writers were gaining fame around the world. Democracy seemed to be working. That same year, Germany was admitted to the League of Nations.

But democracy didn't have deep roots in German soil. Germans were used to a strong central authority. The country could not escape its past. The military continued to have a strong say in running the government.

There was also a problem built into the Weimar Constitution. The document was similar in many ways to the United States Constitution. But there was one huge difference.

Article 48 of the German document allowed the president to suspend the constitution in a time of emergency. That was a dangerous loophole. A weak or power-seeking president could use it to great harm. Article 48 could destroy the constitution itself. It could spell the downfall of the Weimar Republic. ■

In the early years of the Weimar Republic, people often took to the streets to protest. Here, a workers' "Demonstration for Peace" is held in Berlin in 1921.

Hitler Tries Power Grab; Attempted Revolt Fails in Munich

When the shooting was over, 16 Nazis and four policemen were dead.

When the gun went off, Gustav von Kahr shut up fast. About 3,000 people in the beer hall were listening to his speech. They never heard the end of it. Instead, they heard the words of the man with the gun.

Their government was being overthrown, he said. A revolution had come to Germany. The *putsch*—or overthrow—was starting now!

The man's name was Adolf Hitler. At age 34, he was prepared to take control of Germany. His chances seemed good. He had been thinking about a revolution for a long time. In fact, so had many Germans.

When Germany surrendered in 1918, many Germans were upset. They felt they should have fought to the last man. Many of them blamed the new Weimar government for surrendering.

Hitler, who had been a corporal in the German Army, felt betrayed. He felt that his country had been stabbed in the back. He decided to go into politics. Although he had no supporters, he did have a strong belief in himself. Sooner or later, he felt, he would find political backing.

After the war, Hitler stayed in the army. His job was to spy on political groups in Munich. Mostly he was supposed to spy on Communists and Socialists. The army generals were afraid of these Reds, as they were called. The generals didn't want a revolution like the one that occurred in Russia.

While spying, Hitler heard about the German Worker's Party. The members seemed to share his views. They hated Communists, Socialists, and Jews. They also hated democracy. They were the kind of backers Hitler needed, so he joined their group.

A New Name—Nazis

Hitler was a good public speaker. After hearing his speeches, many people joined the party. Soon he formed a small army of bullies and called them "storm troopers." He used them against his political enemies. They broke up meetings, beat people, and even committed murder.

In 1921, after only two years, Hitler became head of the party. He

took the title *Führer*—Leader. He gave the party a new name— National Socialist Workers Party. People began calling Hitler and his followers "Nazis."

Soon Hitler had put together a group of men who understood politics. They were willing to help him reach his goal—Führer of all Germany!

On November 8, 1923, Hitler and his storm troopers went into action. They headed for the beer hall in Munich. Gustav von Kahr was speaking there. Kahr was one of three men who governed the province of Bavaria. The other two Bavarian leaders were also present.

After firing his gun, Hitler went up to the speaker's stand. "The national revolution has begun!" he cried. Hitler told the crowd that he was forming a new government. He said that he would march to Berlin and overthrow the German government.

The three leaders of the Bavarian government pretended to support him. As soon as they could, though, they contacted the police.

The next day Hitler led the Nazis on a march. With him was General Erich Ludendorff, a hero of the Great War. He supported Hitler's views.

The marchers headed for the center of Munich. On the way, they ran into the police. Soon bullets were flying. When the shooting was over, 16 Nazis and 4 policemen were dead. Hitler's *putsch* had failed.

Hitler was found guilty of high treason. The court sentenced him to five years in jail. But he was released after only nine months. He spent the remainder of the decade reorganizing his Nazi party and speaking out against the Weimar government. ■

Adolf Hitler (far left) and several of his Nazi supporters at a meeting in 1924. Hitler's attempted overthrow of the democratic German government was put down by Munich police.

Earthquake Strikes Japan

Thousands Die As Tokyo Burns

Since 1871 lunchtime in Tokyo had always been announced with a bang. Each day at noon a cannon was fired in the palace plaza. But on September 1, 1923, the shot wasn't heard. Instead, the people of Japan's largest city heard only the sickening sounds of disaster.

A minute before noon the great Kanto earthquake struck. The city was filled with the roar of buildings being torn apart. Streets were ripped up. Cars smashed into each other. All the sirens in the city began to wail. The screams and cries of frightened people filled the air.

The people who lived in Tokyo were used to feeling the earth shake. The Kanto Plain where Tokyo is located, is earthquake country. Tiny earthquakes took place often. And there had been a bad one there almost 30 years before. Still, the people weren't ready for this one.

During the first few minutes, a huge temple was knocked down. About 700 people inside were killed. Another 600 people were killed when a tunnel fell in on them. And the worst was yet to come.

No time is a good time for an earthquake. But noon was an especially bad time. All over the city, Japanese women were preparing lunch for their families. Thousands of them used open charcoal fires for cooking. When the earthquake hit, sparks from those fires were sent flying. Many houses were made of wood, so in a short time, thousands of houses went up in flames.

The earthquake also broke gas pipes. That caused explosions and more fires. To make things worse, a strong wind started to blow, and the flames quickly spread.

> "It was meaningless—there were no landmarks, no familiar buildings."

Because the streets were blocked, the city's firemen could do little to help. They couldn't move their trucks. But even if they could, it wouldn't have done much good. Many of the city's water pipes were broken.

All over the city, frightened people ran for their lives. Many tried to find safety near the Samida River. They crowded together in a park by the river bank. But it was no use. No place was safe in Tokyo that day. A whirlwind of fire blew down on them. It burned all the oxygen from the air. About 30,000 people died because they couldn't breathe. Another 800 were killed when the Imperial University Hospital burned.

Landslides and Tidal Waves

The fires continued for three days. The damage was terrible. And fires weren't the only problem. There were also landslides. One pushed a train into the waters of the Sagami Bay. The train's 200 passengers were never seen again.

The earthquake also caused a *tsunami*—a tidal wave. At one point it was more than 30 feet high. When it struck the beach at Kamakura, it drowned 100 people.

The center of the earthquake was in Sagami Bay. Yokohama, on the other side of the bay, was also hit hard. That city, too, was almost totally destroyed. As in Tokyo, the worst damage was caused by fire. In those few days, Yokohama was completely changed. After looking at the destruction from a hill, one man wrote: "It was meaningless—there were no landmarks, no familiar buildings."

The entire world was shocked by the Tokyo disaster. The United

States sent 60 ships with supplies and relief workers. San Francisco had been hit with a terrible earthquake 17 years earlier. At that time the Japanese Red Cross had sent $100,000 in aid. Now the American Red Cross sent $100,000 to Japan. Other countries joined in.

Some of the people who died in Tokyo were Americans. One of them was the U.S. consul. Some members of the Japanese Royal Family died, too. At first, Crown Prince Hirohito thought his parents were killed. All phones were knocked out by the earthquake. So he sent a plane to drop a message on the Royal palace. He asked that a flag be waved if the people inside were still alive. Soon after that, the pilot saw the flag waving. He returned to Hirohito with the good news.

A New Hotel Survives

Because of American Frank Lloyd Wright, a number of lives were saved. He had designed The Imperial Hotel in the center of Tokyo. It had officially opened the day before the earthquake. Wright knew that Tokyo was in an active earthquake area. To make the hotel safe, he tried a new idea. He built a special base for the building. During the earthquake, the hotel rocked like a ship in a storm. But it didn't fall apart. His idea had worked!

The hotel was one of the few large buildings left standing. It became the headquarters for giving aid to the city. It was used as a giant kitchen and as a hospital.

In all, more than 140,000 people died during the Kanto earthquake. Most of them died in fires. A half-million people were injured. And nearly 700,000 houses were destroyed. ∎

Laborers clear debris from the streets of Tokyo after the devastating earthquake that rocked the city on September 1, 1923.

U.S. Says No to League of Nations

"The world must be made safe for democracy." Those were the words President Wilson used when the United States entered the Great War. When the war was over, Wilson had a plan for lasting peace. It was made up of Fourteen Points. Each one was aimed at bringing a sense of fair play to world politics.

The last of Wilson's Fourteen Points was the most important one. It called for the formation of a League of Nations. Wilson felt that nations would avoid wars only if they could meet together.

In the summer of 1919, the Treaty of Paris was drawn up. It officially ended the Great War. It also set up a plan for Wilson's League of Nations. Representatives from the European countries knew their people would support such a league. And President Wilson was confident the American people would support

An editorial cartoon showing President Woodrow Wilson trying to get his peace treaty through "ratification rapids"—the dangerous waters of the United States Senate.

A political cartoonist condemned the U.S. Senate for refusing to ratify the Peace Treaty in March 1920.

it as well. He returned to the United States with high hopes that the U.S. Senate would agree to the treaty. If that happened, the United States could join the League.

But Wilson was greatly disappointed when he arrived at home. Many people in the United States didn't like the idea of Wilson's League. A certain part of the League plan caused major problems. That was Article Ten. That article concerned threats to any member nation of the League. If such threats were made, the other members were supposed to aid the threatened nation.

America had seen the results of war. A million Americans had fought in the Great War. Millions of others had lost family and friends because of it. In the beginning, many had supported America's fighting in the war. But they hadn't realized what the cost in money and lives would be.

Now many Americans wanted to stay out of all wars. And they didn't want to have anything to do with Europe and its problems anymore. To them, Article Ten seemed to invite trouble.

Wilson tried to convince Americans that peace could be kept only with the League of Nations. He said that wars start when nations can't talk with each other about their problems.

Under the rules of the U.S. Constitution, Wilson needed the Senate's support to get America into the League. That was a big problem for him. He had made a lot of political enemies in the country.

After the United States had entered the fighting in Europe, Wilson had promised not to bring politics into the war effort. But in 1918, Democrat Wilson had made many speeches supporting other Democrats. He had said that if Democrats were elected, the war would end sooner. That had angered many Republicans—and they hadn't forgotten it. Now they had a chance to get even.

Massachusetts Republican Senator Henry Cabot Lodge opposed ⇨

> ## "We seek no part in directing the destinies of the world."

Senator William Borah of Idaho was one of the leading opponents of America's entry into the League of Nations.

Wilson. He said he liked the idea of a League of Nations. But he didn't like the way Wilson had helped set it up. The fact was, Lodge didn't want Wilson to get credit for the League.

Two other senators fought Wilson even harder. They were California's Hiram Johnson and Idaho's William Borah. Both were powerful Republican Senate leaders. They didn't want America to be part of *any* kind of League of Nations. Because of Lodge, Borah, and Johnson, the Senate turned against Wilson. The three senators also turned many other Americans against him.

Wilson put up a strong fight. He made speeches around the country,

All of Wilson's talk was in vain. America didn't want to hear what he said.

The first session of the League of Nations was held at its headquarters in Geneva, Switzerland, in January 1920. Forty-two nations joined the League and sent their representatives. The United States was not one of them.

trying to convince Americans to support the League. But the fight was too much for him. In September 1919, he suffered a stroke. He returned home from his trip a very sick man.

Wilson Stands Firm

There were some senators on Wilson's side. They told him that he should give in on a few points. But Wilson refused. He wanted the Senate to join the League according to the plan he'd brought back from Paris.

That pleased his opponents. They were afraid the League might be accepted if Wilson backed down a little. But now, they felt, it wouldn't have a chance. They were right. In November 1919, the Senate voted against the treaty.

President Wilson had created the League of Nations. And now his own country had refused to become a member! The Senate voted on the treaty once more in March 1920. And once more it was defeated.

Wilson and his supporters tried one last time to get approval for the League. James M. Cox was the Democratic candidate for president in 1920. If he won, he said, he would again push for America's entrance into the League. Sick as he was, Wilson tried to help Cox. But it was no use.

Republican Warren Harding was elected. He hadn't said much about the League before the election. Afterwards though, he made it clear where he stood. He said: "We seek no part in directing the destinies of the world."

As far as America was concerned, the League was a dead issue.

Wilson never fully recovered his health. In February 1924 he died, a defeated man. He'd warned that another world war was not far off. He'd said that only the League of Nations could prevent it. But all his talk was in vain. America didn't want to hear him. ■

Demonstrators took to the streets of Paris in 1925 to support the cause of Sacco and Vanzetti.

Worldwide Support for Sacco and Vanzetti

Embattled Immigrants Fight Murder Charges

How could a country like the United States be so unfair? That's what people around the world were asking.

They were talking about the case of Sacco and Vanzetti. A jury had found Nicola Sacco and Bartolomeo Vanzetti guilty of murder. The two had been sentenced to death. But millions of people thought they were innocent. And there seemed to be a lot of evidence to support that feeling.

It all began near Boston in the spring of 1920. A shoe factory had been robbed and two men killed. The police had no suspects. With little evidence to go on, they blamed Sacco and Vanzetti.

Both men swore they were innocent. They had witnesses to back up their stories. But that didn't help them. The facts in this case weren't the most important thing. Fear and prejudice played a much larger part.

At that time, many Americans were very fearful of Communists. In Russia, Communists had overthrown the government. That frightened many people in the United States—especially people in power. They didn't want a revolution in America. But that was just what the Communists and Socialists in America wanted. Or so the people in power said. Free speech or not, those in power wanted to silence these people.

Nicola Sacco, 29, worked in a shoe factory. Bartolomeo Vanzetti, 33, sold fish for a living. The two friends were Italian immigrants. They were known as peaceful men, opposed to war. They were also anarchists, people who believed in a free society without governments. Many people didn't like anarchists any more than Communists. One of these people was the judge at their trial, Webster Thayer.

Judge Thayer was against Sacco and Vanzetti from the start. The foreman of the jury, it turned out, was also against them. He didn't care if they were guilty or innocent. They were radicals. That was all that mattered. Before the trial he had said, "They ought to hang anyway."

The trial began in May of 1921 and lasted six weeks. The evidence against Sacco and Vanzetti was weak. Many people testified they were with both men when the robbery took place. They said there was no way they could have done it. Still, they were found guilty. And Judge Thayer sentenced them to death.

But that wasn't the end of the case. For the next six years, lawyers tried to get the verdict overturned. During that time, the two men were kept in prison. While the lawyers worked for their freedom, more information came out. Witnesses against them admitted they had been wrong. The prejudice of Judge Thayer was revealed. And it was shown that the government had misrepresented the evidence.

People around the world protested. America was supposed to be the land of justice. Why was the government mistreating these two men?

Protests Around the World

There were big protest meetings held in Asia, Africa, Europe, and South America. Workers went on strike to protest the injustice. They threw stones at American embassies.

Finally, Sacco and Vanzetti's lawyers had gone as far as they could go. They had tried everything. Only one person could save the accused men. That was the governor of Massachusetts, Alvin Tufts Fuller. If he thought they had been convicted unfairly, he could commute their death sentence.

Before he decided Sacco and Vanzetti's fate, Fuller appointed a commission. Three men were named ⇨

Nicola Sacco (right) and Bartolomeo Vanzetti. Thousands of people in America and around the world believed they were unjustly tried and convicted of murder.

to review the facts. The commission was headed up by Lawrence A. Lowell, the president of Harvard University. Another commission member was Samuel W. Stratton, president of Massachusetts Institute of Technology (M.I.T.). The third member was Robert A. Grant, a former judge.

The commissioners listened to many people who had been at the trial. Some of the witnesses against Sacco and Vanzetti changed their stories. Eighteen people swore that Vanzetti couldn't have possibly been at the holdup. They said he was selling them fish in Plymouth when it happened.

At the time of the trial, neither Sacco nor Vanzetti spoke English

well. The man who translated for them had made mistakes. Because he had translated their words incorrectly, he had hurt their case. The commissioners also heard that the jury foreman had been prejudiced.

There was much evidence that the trial had been unfair. But none of it seemed to make a difference. Lowell himself seemed prejudiced. At one point he said a witness for the men was lying. He said he had evidence that the man's story wasn't true. As it turned out, Lowell himself was lying. He wanted to scare the man into taking back what he said. The next day the man proved he was telling the truth.

Lowell apologized then. But he erased the story from the commis-

sion's final report. He didn't want everyone to know he had lied.

The new evidence in favor of Sacco and Vanzetti did them no good. The commission paid no attention to it. Lowell *did* mention that Judge Thayer had made bigoted statements. But, he said, Thayer made them on his own time. It had nothing to do with the trial. As far as the commission was concerned, the trial had been fair.

Governor Fuller agreed. He said that the sentence would be carried out. Early on August 23, 1927, Sacco and Vanzetti died in the electric chair.

Thousands of people around the world and at home mourned. Many felt that justice had died along with Sacco and Vanzetti. ∎

Condemned Men Speak to the World

"Judge Thayer know all my life, and he know that I am never guilty, never—not yesterday, nor today, nor forever."

Nicola Sacco

"If it had not been for this thing, I might have lived out my life talking at street corners to scorning men. I might have died, unmarked, unknown, a failure. Now we are not a failure. This is our career and our triumph. Never in our full life can we hope to do such work for tolerance, for justice, for man's understanding of man, as now we do by accident. Our words—our lives—our pains— nothing! The taking of our lives— lives of a good shoemaker and a poor fish peddler—all! That last moment belongs to us—that agony is our triumph."

Bartolomeo Vanzetti

President Warren Harding brought many of his friends to Washington with him. Some of them betrayed his friendship.

Warren Harding

A Short, Unhappy Term as President

In the election of 1920, Warren Harding made sense to many Americans. The Great War had given America enough excitement. Woodrow Wilson had wanted to bring peace to the world. Instead he had brought the United States into the war.

Many Americans felt betrayed. Wilson had been a college president before becoming president of the United States. Clearly he was an intelligent man. But he still got the country mixed up in Europe's war.

Maybe the country didn't need a president who was that well educated. That's what some Americans thought. They wanted an average man. Someone like the man next door. In the 1920 presidential election, that's what they got.

The Republican party chose ⇨

"Harding is no world-beater. But he's the best of the second-raters."

Senator Warren Harding as their candidate. One reason he was chosen was that he was so ordinary. Harding had grown up in a small town in Ohio. He had led a "normal" life before running for president. And as a candidate, he promised to return the country to that "normalcy." No more meddling in Europe's problems. No more fighting other people's wars.

Harding hadn't really wanted to be president. But many Republicans had talked him into running. A lot of them felt they could use him to help themselves. They were sure he'd be elected. He was a handsome man. He was open and friendly. As a senator he had done very little—his record was neither good nor bad.

Ohio Friend Is Pleased

Senator Brandegee of Connecticut put it well. "Harding is no world-beater. But he is the best of the second-raters."

One man was especially pleased with Harding's record. That was Harry Daugherty, a lawyer from Ohio. He had been guiding Harding's political career for several years. He thought Harding would be the ideal man to run for president.

In the November election Harding ran against Democrat James M. Cox. Former President Wilson supported Cox. That support probably hurt Cox more than it helped him. When the results were in, Harding had gotten almost twice as many votes as Cox.

Once Harding was elected, he had to pick his cabinet and other advisors. Some of the men he chose were outstanding. Herbert Hoover became his Secretary of Commerce. Charles Evans Hughes was chosen to be Secretary of State. And Andrew Mellon was picked to be Secretary of the Treasury. All three had won reputations for honesty and hard work.

But Harding also picked men because they were his pals. He named his friend Harry Daugherty to

be Attorney General. And he made Albert Fall his Secretary of the Interior. Many people thought they weren't very well qualified. But Harding felt comfortable with them.

The Poker Cabinet

One of Harding's joys was playing cards. Most nights in the White House, Harding and a group of friends played poker. The men who played became known as Harding's "Poker Cabinet." They weren't part of his administration. Still, many times Harding took their advice. And it was often bad.

Among the regular players was Colonel Charles Forbes. He later went to jail for cheating veterans. Another frequent visitor to the White House was Mort Mortimer. He filled a special role among Harding's friends. With Prohibition in effect during the decade, it was illegal to buy or sell liquor. But the men in the "Poker Cabinet" liked to drink. So Mortimer supplied the illegal liquor.

By 1923 it became obvious to many people that Harding had chosen some bad advisors. Stories about government corruption were becoming more than rumors. The Congress was getting ready to investigate many of Harding's friends.

Harding himself was in the wrong job. Being president was too much for him to handle. He once said, "I am a man of limited talents from a small town." No one argued that.

By the summer of 1923, Harding was worried. He knew by then that many of his friends had used their government connections and made illegal business deals. He was actually getting sick over it. He took a vacation to get away from Washington for a while. But in San Francisco, his doctors found he was suffering from pneumonia. There, on August 2, he died. In a way, he was lucky. Death spared him from seeing so many of his friends disgraced. ∎

Teapot Dome

Oil Lease Scandal Rocks Washington

President Harding liked Albert Fall. When they had been fellow senators, they used to play poker together. So when Harding became president he named Fall his Secretary of the Interior. After his election, Harding rewarded many of his friends with government jobs. Some of them, like Fall, didn't have much experience. But Harding trusted them just the same.

In 1921 Fall asked Harding to sign an order. It had something to do with oil. Harding didn't know too much about it. But he felt he could trust his poker-playing pal.

The order gave Fall control of three big government oil fields. One was at Buena Vista, California. Another was at Elk Hills, California. The third was located at Teapot Dome, Wyoming.

Since 1909 the government had been keeping oil there on reserve. ⇨

A political cartoon from the mid-1920s after the Teapot Dome scandal was revealed.

It was to be used for an emergency. Until Harding signed the order, the Navy had been in charge. Once the order was signed though, Fall and the Department of Interior took over.

Fall had friends in the oil business. One friend was Harry F. Sinclair, who owned Mammoth Oil Company. Acting secretly, Fall leased the Teapot Dome field to him. He also leased the Elk Hills Reserve to Edward F. Doheny's Pan-American Company. Doheny was another friend. That lease was also made in secret.

The plan was that the two oil companies would protect the oil. They would have the right to sell some of it. But they would also keep a supply on hand. In case of war America could count on having oil.

Some people wondered why the deals were made in secret. Why hadn't other companies had a chance to bid on the leases? Fall said it was because of national security. These were war reserves. The deals had to be secret to protect America. Fall said the arrangement was in the best interest of the country. The oil companies would benefit and the government would benefit.

"Gifts and Loans"

What Fall didn't say was that he would benefit as well—in fact *very* well. Fall had received a "gift" of $260,000 from Sinclair. In addition, Doheny had loaned Fall $100,000. The "loan" was interest free. And Fall had put up no security for it.

Doheny later told investigators that there was nothing wrong with the loan. He knew that Fall needed money to buy a ranch. The payment wasn't meant to influence the oil leases. But most people found that story hard to believe. It looked very much like Fall had taken a bribe.

After many investigations, Fall was put on trial. He was found guilty and sentenced to a year in prison. The strange thing was, both Doheny and Sinclair went free. Fall was found guilty of taking bribes. But for some reason, the men who bribed him were found innocent! Later Sinclair was sentenced to prison on other charges.

The "Teapot Dome" scandal involved many people in the oil business. It also involved the Republican National Committee. By the time the full story came out, President Harding had already died. But for an administration that had been smeared by other scandals, Teapot Dome became the biggest stain of all.

■

> Some people wondered why the deals were made in secret.

Secretary of the Interior Albert Fall used his position to reward friends with government oil leases. In return, Fall received more than $100,000 in bribes.

Four Years of Coolidge Prosperity

John Coolidge climbed the farm-house stairs and shook his son Calvin awake. It was early in the morning of August 3, 1923. Even the chickens in Vermont were still sleeping. John knew his son loved his sleep. Still, he had some important news to give him. President Harding had died the night before. That meant that Calvin, America's vice president, was about to take charge of the nation.

The Coolidges wasted no time. John was a notary public. A little before 4 A.M. he swore his son into office.

Calvin Coolidge later said he had only one regret that morning. He wished that his mother were still alive. "Some way, that morning, she seemed very near to me," he said.

Coolidge's mother had shaped his life. She had brought him up to be honest and hard working. He went to church. He didn't drink. He studied hard in school. Those lessons would pay off in the end. He'd bring no scandal to the White House. There'd be nothing like Harding's "Poker Cabinet" while Coolidge was in office. He didn't gamble either.

When Coolidge took office the country was in pretty good shape. There were scandals left over from Harding's administration. But Coolidge wasn't part of them.

When Coolidge took office most Americans didn't know very much about him. He had never been a big talker. He had earned the nickname "Silent Cal." His wife told the story of how he had accepted the offer to run as vice president. Someone telephoned him to say he had been nominated. Mrs. Coolidge asked if he would accept. "I suppose I shall have to," he said. And that was that.

Coolidge had never been one to get excited. And that didn't change once he was president. As far as he

President Calvin Coolidge. He believed that "the business of America is business."

was concerned, the country was doing fine.

It was hard to argue that point. The Great War was long since over. Business was good. America didn't seem likely to get involved again with Europe's problems.

A Man of Few Words

When the 1924 elections came, Coolidge took it easy. That was his style, and he saw no need to change it. John Davis was the Democrat's candidate for president. He traveled around the country looking for votes. Coolidge stayed in the White House. The Republican slogan was "Keep Cool and Keep Coolidge." He *was* cool and calm. And that's what the country wanted. He beat Davis soundly.

Many stories were told about his reputation for being a man of few words. Once a woman tried to start a conversation with him. She told him she had made a bet with a friend. "I bet that I could make you say more than two words," she teased.

"You lose," Coolidge said, and turned away.

Neither talk nor action suited Coolidge. While in office, he did very little. He had a rocking chair put on the White House front porch. He liked to relax there. He also liked to relax in his office. He often put his feet up on his desk and fell asleep.

As far as Coolidge was concerned, the president's job wasn't that important. He felt that business-men ran the country. And he thought that was the way it should be. He once said, "The business of America is business."

Business did seem to be faring very well during his term of office. As 1928 approached, America was in the middle of "Coolidge Prosperity." It looked like Coolidge could be a sure winner in the upcoming election.

Instead he made an announcement that startled Americans. "I do not choose to run for office," he said. "Silent Cal" had had enough. It was time to retire to the farm in Vermont.

■

Clarence Darrow (left) and William Jennings Bryan clashed fiercely in 1925 in a battle over the teaching of evolution.

Evolution vs. The Bible

Legal Giants Clash in Scopes "Monkey Trial"

In the spring of 1925, John Scopes knew he would be arrested. That's what he was hoping for. The young Dayton, Tennessee biology teacher knew what the law was. But he also thought that, in this case, the law was based on ignorance.

The law was the Butler Act, passed a few months earlier. It outlawed the teaching of Darwin's Theory of Evolution in Tennessee schools.

The law was passed to please Fundamentalists. They were people who believed in an exact interpretation of the Bible. Because of that, they were opposed to Darwin's Theory of Evolution. It denied the theory of Divine Creation as taught in the Bible. Evolution taught that man had descended from a lower order of animals. Not only was it wrong, the Fundamentalists thought— it was sinful!

Once the lawmakers had gone on record against sin, they thought the matter was ended. Most weren't concerned about the Butler Act. But Roger Baldwin was. He was head of the American Civil Liberties Union, the ACLU. He thought the law was unconstitutional, and that it should be challenged in court. He announced that the ACLU would pay the cost of a trial.

George Rappelyea, a young

Dayton businessman, heard about the ACLU offer. He knew that young John Scopes might be interested. When he explained the situation, Scopes was indeed interested. He said he *already* was teaching evolution in his high school classes. He'd try to help overturn the law.

Rappelyea explained that Scopes would first have to *ask* to be arrested. That worried Scopes. He was afraid it might hurt his career. But Rappelyea said no. It would be a quiet legal argument he said. The lawyers would discuss their ideas before a judge. It would be mostly a paper battle of legal briefs. In that case, Scopes said, he'd go along with the plan.

The battle to come, however, was anything but quiet. It brought two legal giants to the Dayton courthouse. It also brought newspaper reporters from around the world to the little Tennessee town.

Clarence Darrow was defending John Scopes. Darrow was America's most famous criminal lawyer. He was also an avowed agnostic, someone who believes God's existence cannot be proved. He was an opponent of Fundamentalism, and all organized religion. For the first time in his career, he took on a case without charge.

William Jennings Bryan was a household name. He had run for president three times. He had been Secretary of State under Woodrow Wilson. A brilliant speaker, his attacks on "nonbelievers" were well known. He had decided to come to Dayton on his own to help prosecute the case against Scopes.

Darrow against Bryan promised to be an exciting match. And it was. They went at each other like a cat and a dog.

The trial was set for July 25. From the beginning, Darrow knew there would be problems. Fundamentalism was popular in Dayton. Judge J. Raulston had a sign behind his bench that said: "READ YOUR BIBLE!" Darrow knew that a   ⇨

A packed Dayton, Tennessee courtroom crowd hears testimony in the trial against high school teacher John Scopes (seated, leaning forward with arms folded).

victory in Dayton wasn't likely. Still, he hoped to show the error of outlawing nonreligious teachings in the public schools.

Darrow tried to show that the Butler Act wasn't scientific. But time after time, Judge Raulston overruled him. Darrow tried to present scientists who traced man's history back 600,000 years. But the judge wouldn't allow their testimony. The Bible said man was created 6,000 years ago. To Judge Raulston, that was that.

The defense said the issue was whether or not evolution was scientifically true. The prosecution disagreed. It said that the only issue was whether or not Scopes broke the law. The judge took the prosecution's side. For a while it looked as though the trial would be over quickly.

A Surprising Witness

Then the defense made a surprising move. Darrow called for William Jennings Bryan to take the stand. The trial was boiling down to a standoff between Darrow and Bryan. This is what the newspaper reporters had

been waiting for. It was what everyone had been waiting for. This was going to be a show!

Judge Raulston thought so, too. He moved the trial out of the courthouse and onto the lawn. Outside there would be room for everybody to watch the fireworks.

Bryan was eager to take the stand. He thought he could defend the Bible as literal history. But he was wrong. Time after time, he had to slip around Darrow's questions.

Darrow: Do you believe Joshua made the sun stand still?

Bryan: I believe what the Bible says.

Darrow: Now, Mr. Bryan, have you ever pondered what would have happened to the earth if it had stood still?

Bryan: No, the God I believe in could have taken care of that, Mr. Darrow.

Later Darrow asked Bryan about the snake in the Garden of Eden.

Darrow: Do you think the snake crawled on his belly as a punishment?

Bryan: I believe that.

Darrow: Have you any idea how the snake moved around before that time?

Bryan: No, sir.

Darrow: Do you know whether he walked on his tail or not?

Bryan: No, sir. I have no way to know.

At times the two men actually shook their fists at each other.

At one point Darrow asked, "You don't care how old earth is, how old man is, and how long the animals have been here?"

"No," Bryan answered. "I am not much interested in that."

Bryan was digging himself in deeper. Finally the judge called a halt to his testimony. He said it could serve no purpose. The only question was, had Scopes broken the law? The jury quicky reached a decision. He had. Judge Raulston fined Scopes $100, the minimum amount.

Scopes's ideas weren't changed by the outcome of the case. He said, "I feel I have been convicted of an unjust statute. I will continue to oppose this law in any way I can."

The legal defeat didn't bother Darrow. He had felt all along that he couldn't win in Dayton. Now he hoped to take the case all the way to the Supreme Court.

But he didn't get the chance. The judge had made an error in the trial. The law said he should have let the jury set the fine. Scopes's conviction was overturned because of that error.

The case was finished. Neither side had won a clear victory. Still, the overall victory went to Scopes and students of science. People from around the world read reports of the Dayton trial. Bryan's lack of scientific knowledge gave support to the opposition. He had made a laughing stock of ignorance. ∎

Charles Darwin. A Tennessee law banned the teaching of his theory of evolution.

Billy Mitchell

A War Hero Is Court-Martialed

In September 1925, the American government decided to court-martial "Billy" Mitchell. The public was shocked and the military was rocked.

This was no routine trial. Army pilot William "Billy" Mitchell was a high-ranking officer and a decorated hero of the Great War. Mitchell had been the first American to fly over enemy lines. While commanding aviation units, he had continued to fly missions himself. And he had earned every one of his medals.

In 1920, at the age of 41, he was already a brigadier general. His future looked good. Still, Mitchell wasn't happy. He didn't like the look of America's fighting forces. During the war, he had learned the value of airplanes. Then, they were used mostly for observation. They were also used in "dog fights," matching one pilot against another. Airplanes did some bombing, but not much.

That would change, Mitchell thought. He believed that airplanes were the weapons of the future. He also believed the country should have an Air Force, separate from the Army and Navy. His superiors disagreed. They felt wars would always be fought on land and sea. That was the business of the Army and the Navy. Sure, some airplanes were needed for observation—but not many. Besides, they cost too much. They told him to forget his ideas.

But Mitchell wouldn't keep quiet. He said America would be defeated if it didn't have a separate air force. He wrote a book about it. He wrote articles about it in newspapers and magazines. He even made speeches around the country. Air warfare was here to stay, he said. To prove it, he showed in tests that bombs could sink battleships.

By 1925 Mitchell's superiors were fed up. They lowered his rank and gave him a less important job.

After a Navy dirigible crashed in a storm, Mitchell spoke up again. He accused the War and Navy departments of not caring about safety. He said their behavior was close to treason. That was too much. He had ignored all warnings about the danger of attacking his superiors and the government. Now he was faced with a military trial—a court-martial.

But even that didn't silence him. During the trial he charged that the country was unprepared for the next war. He warned of dangers ahead. Those statements only made matters worse. Mitchell was found guilty of making statements that hurt the military. He was suspended from the service without pay for five years. Now Mitchell felt he had no choice. He resigned from the Army completely. Out of uniform, Mitchell continued to push for a strong National defense.

Many people agreed with Mitchell's beliefs. Still, they felt he should have obeyed orders. They said he should have kept quiet and let others state his ideas.

It turned out that his efforts weren't entirely wasted. In 1926 the Army Air Corps was established. It must have given Mitchell some sense of satisfaction. Someone must have been listening after all. ■

The Charleston
The Dance of the Decade

Jazz was the music of the '20s—wild and free. In jazz, young people found the freedom they'd been looking for. One jazz dance stood out above all others—the Charleston.

Although new to white America, it was not a new dance. Negroes had been doing a dance like the Charleston for a long time. It was rooted in a dance of Africa's Ashanti people.

In 1923, the Charleston was seen in the all-black musical *Runnin' Wild*. It was a special hit with Bee Jackson, a white dancer. After seeing the show, she went to Lyda Webb, the director. She asked to learn the dance, and Webb agreed to teach her.

Soon, Jackson was doing the Charleston for white audiences in New York. It was a big hit with them, too. It became popular all over the city. By 1925 it was the most popular dance in America. Charleston contests were being held across the country.

People liked the Charleston for two main reasons. It was fun to watch, and fun to do. With elbows out and knees in, the dancers seemed filled with joy. The jazz music they danced to set the mood. It was definitely upbeat.

Some people were against the Charleston. To them it was just another sign of the times. It showed how wild the young people had become.

Boston City Council members tried to ban the dance in 1925. But not because they thought it was immoral. A tragedy had just taken place there. More than 40 people had been killed at the Pickwick Club. The old building had caved in while people were dancing the Charleston. Fortunately for the dance lovers, the city council didn't succeed.

Hollywood quickly took notice of America's love of the Charleston. It was a featured dance in many movies. Some stars owed their fame to the dance. Actress Ginger Rogers was billed as "Queen of the Charleston." Star Joan Crawford got her start in *Our Dancing Daughters*. The daughters, of course, danced the Charleston.

The Charleston wasn't the only big dance of the 1920s. There was the romantic Tango. There was the daring Shimmy. But the Charleston was the leader. It was the perfect dance for the wild and woolly 1920s.

The Charleston. With elbows out and knees in, the dancers seemed filled with joy.

The Marathon Craze

They Danced Until They Dropped

Marathon Dancing. Often one dancer would have to hold up a sleeping partner.

In the 1920s people were kicking up their heels. Dances like the Charleston were popular all across the country. High-spirited young people wanted to dance until they dropped. And that's just what some of them did!

They were the ones who took part in marathon dances. It was a chance for couples to win money. All they had to do was dance longer than all the other couples who were dancing. They didn't even have to dance, really. They just had to hold onto each other and keep moving.

At the start of the marathon dance it seemed like fun. But as the hours slowly passed, dancing became torture. Often, one dancer would have to hold up a sleeping partner. That was allowed. As long as one of them kept moving, they stayed in the marathon.

The people who promoted marathons said the events were healthy. But others didn't think so. To prove their point, they would bring up Homer Morehouse. In 1923 Homer danced without a break for 87 hours. It wasn't a record for marathon dancing. But he did set a record of sorts. At the end of 87 hours, he dropped dead. He was the first fatality of the marathon-dancing craze.

After that the rules were changed. Dancers were allowed to take rest breaks. Still, the marathons were exhausting affairs. Because of Morehouse's death, some states outlawed marathons. But in 1928, they were still legal in New York. In June of that year, the "Dance Derby of the Century" began. The Derby was put on by Milton Crandall. He'd been a Hollywood promoter. He had a good eye for what the public wanted. The dance was held in New York's Madison Square Garden. What made it so popular was the prize money. The winning couple would get $5,000.

The rules were simple. Couples danced an hour and then took a fifteen minute break. All they had to do was to hang onto each other and keep moving. If either person's knee touched the floor, that was it. The couple was out of the money.

At the start of the Derby there were 91 couples. After five days, more than 60 had dropped out. The dance dragged on. And Crandall made money. People were paying $2.20 a ticket just to watch. After 20 days, a judge ordered Crandall to stop the marathon. He said the dancers' healths were in danger. There were still nine couples left.

During the marathon, Crandall took in $121,000. He said that his profit was only $25,000 after expenses. The nine couples who finished divided the $5,000 prize. That came to about $278 for each person. They had danced for almost three weeks straight—and had earned less than 58 cents an hour!

A Dancer's First Wish After a Marathon

"I'd like to take a shower and go to a real dance with lots of swell partners."—Mary "Hercules Mary" Promitis, one of the finishers in the Dance Derby of the Century.

41

Some speakeasies featured music and entertainment as well as illegal liquor. Others, like the one pictured here, were simply bars for drinking.

Prohibition Or Not— Americans Keep on Drinking

Prohibition began in 1920. That year all manufacture, sale, and transportation of alcoholic beverages (except for use as medicine) became illegal. Saloons and bars all across the country went out of business. But almost as soon as the saloons and bars closed the first, "speak-easies" opened. Ten years later, they're still going strong.

What are "speakeasies"? They are places where a person can sit and listen to some music, dance with a pretty gal or handsome guy—and drink alcoholic beverages! Of course, that means that anyone operating a speakeasy, or caught drinking in one, is breaking the law. But that fact hasn't stopped much of the American public during the past decade.

It is impossible to tell how many speakeasies there are in the country. But one estimate in 1929 listed at least 32,000 of them in New York City alone! Some of them are well-known places such as Texas Guinan's, Jack and Charlie's, and Belle Livingston's Country Club.

A Speakeasy is often located behind a "front." In other words, a legal business or house conceals an illegal speakeasy located behind or below it. Getting in is pretty simple— if you know how. Often a customer just rings a bell. Then when someone inside opens a door panel to see who's there, the customer says a password like, "Joe sent me."

Despite being "secret" places, the locations of many speakeasies are known to the authorities. So how do these law-breaking saloons stay in business if the police know their whereabouts? Simple—the owners pay off the police to stay away. And that has made everybody happy— owners, customers, and the police.

A Very Profitable Trade

Prohibition was big business during the 1920s. "Bootleggers" smuggled liquor into the country from Canada and other foreign countries. They supplied liquor to the speakeasies and anyone else who was willing to pay. Illegal booze became a very, very profitable trade. In 1926 alone, the illegal liquor trade had made bootleggers $3.5 billion.

The government did try to crack down on all this illegal bootlegging and drinking. By the late 1920s the FBI and the Coast Guard were arresting an average of 75,000 people a year for Prohibition violations. But there just weren't enough law enforcement people to deal with the situation. And there was another problem. Many officials knew they could make a lot more money in bribes than from their regular salaries. In 1928 alone, the Treasury Department fired 706 of its own Prohibition agents and prosecuted 257 for taking bribes.

So far Prohibition has proved just one thing: What some people want is not what all people want. Despite Congress's passing of the 18th Amendment, many Americans have gone right on drinking. ∎

Getting Paid For Just Sitting Around

In 1924 Alvin "Shipwreck" Kelly climbed up a flagpole and sat there. He sat there, and he sat there. In fact, he sat there for 13 hours and 13 minutes. "That," he said later, "is because 13 is my favorite number."

It didn't seem to make much sense. For that matter, Shipwreck's whole career didn't make much sense. But it made him a living. During the 1920s he was America's best known flagpole sitter.

These were strange times. People were paying to see other people dance until they dropped. Former sailor Kelly figured they'd probably pay to see a man sitting down. If his chair was atop a fifty-foot flagpole, that is. He was right. People did pay to see him. And the pay was great. In 1929 he earned $29,000. That year he put in 145 days of sitting time.

Hotels often hired Kelly to promote business. Whenever he climbed a flagpole, the newspapers reported it. And the hotel got wide publicity. Crowds would stand in the street staring up at him. Viewers could also go up on the roof for a closer look. The rooftop view would cost them 50 cents.

One time a young woman wanted to get even closer to Kelly than that. She got a rope lift to the top of the pole. When she and Shipwreck met, they liked each other. As soon as he climbed down from his perch, they got married.

The chair he used for flagpole sitting was comfortable and safe. It was rubber padded and strapped to the ball of the flagpole. There were holes bored in the seat. He put his thumbs in these holes to hold himself steady while he was sleeping. He also had stirrups attached to the pole to anchor his feet.

In 1927 Kelly set a record in St. Louis. He sat on a flagpole for thirteen days. During that time he drank only coffee. He said it proved you could live on coffee. That was because he was getting money from a coffee company. The truth was, he never did eat while he was aloft. He just drank liquids, which were sent up in a bucket.

Kelly claimed he got his nickname because he had lived through a shipwreck. Some people gave another story to explain his name. Kelly had been an unsuccessful boxer for a while. He was so bad, they said that most of his fights were just about "shipwrecks."

Kelly had another name for himself that no one argued with. He liked to call himself "the luckiest fool alive." Many times he pushed his luck. Once, while pole sitting, he almost froze to death in a storm. He chipped the ice off his body with an ax. But he stayed aloft.

During the decade there were other flagpole sitters, such as "Hold 'em Joe" Powers. But Shipwreck was the champ. He was a man who took pride in his work.

Sure, he was always sitting down on the job. But that's what he was paid for! ■

Alvin "Shipwreck" Kelly hard at "work," high atop the St. Francis Hotel in Newark, N.J.

October 1929. An anxious crowd gathers across from the New York Stock Exchange on Wall Street during the worst market crash in history.

Wall Street Crashes
Many Investors Wiped Out

September 13, 1929, was a day to remember on Wall Street. It was the last good day the stock market would see in the 1920s.

Some people had thought the market would never stop climbing. But sooner or later, bull markets always do. On September 13, the market had gone as high as it would go.

For the next month, stock prices jumped up and down. Something was going on in the market. Just what it was, no one was sure. Then came October 24—"Black Thursday."

The day before, the average stock price had dropped 31 points. On the 24th, people were nervous. At first, prices stayed up. Finally, though, nervousness turned to panic.

Everybody wanted to sell. The stock average dropped like a rock. In one day the market went crazy.

Many people had bought stocks on margin. That meant they had to put up only 10% of the stock's value in cash. They could pay the rest later. When the market began to drop though, the margin payments became due. To get money, many people had to sell their stocks. But as prices dropped, they lost money. Many were wiped out.

That Thursday, almost 13 million shares were traded. It was the busiest day the market had ever seen. The following Tuesday the panic was even worse. More than 16 million shares were traded.

The crash took a lot of people

by surprise. But there were some who expected it. Businessman Roger W. Babson had warned of it a month eariler. "There is a crash coming, and it may be a terrific one," he had written. He added that the market might drop as many as 80 points.

The business journal *Barron's Weekly* laughed at him. They called him a "scaremonger." The *New York Times* attacked Babson and others like him. They said such people were "trying to discredit or stop American prosperity."

As it turned out, the crash was even worse than Babson had predicted. The market dropped 80 points on October 28 alone. By the end of 1929, the value of all the stocks on the exchange had dropped 40%.

Bull Market Promised Easy Money For All

"Everybody Ought to Be Rich." That was the title of an article published in *The Ladies' Home Journal* in the 1920s. It was written by businessman John J. Raskob. The way to get rich, he said, was by buying stocks. Coming from him, it sounded like good advice. After all, Raskob was the vice-president of General Motors.

In 1929 stock prices were rising. If you bought a stock for $100 in March, it might be worth $120 in April. When prices rise that quickly, it's called a "bull market."

As stock prices rose, more people got interested in the market. Some had never bought stocks before. But investing in the market looked too good to pass up. It seemed like such an easy way to make money.

Many people bought stock with borrowed money. That was called "buying on margin." It worked like this. Say a stock sold for $100 a share. You only had to put up $10 to buy a share. You still owed $90, but you didn't have to pay it right away.

If the price rose to $120, you could sell the stock. Then you could pay the $90. You'd make a $20 profit. And all you had to invest was $10. It sounded like a great way to double your money.

But, if the price fell to $80, there was a problem. The people who let you buy on margin got nervous. They'd demand that you pay the $90. If you didn't have the money, you might have to sell the stock. But of course, you'd only get $80 in return for it.

Then you'd lose the $10 you invested. You'd also lose another $10 to make up the difference between the $80 you received and the $90 you owed.

That's the way hundreds of thousands of people bought stocks during the 1920s. While the market continued to climb, things were fine. But when it came crashing down in October 1929, all those people had to find money to pay off their margins. Many of them didn't have it. And of course, they'd invested a lot more money than $10. ∎

Many people lost all their savings. But even those who didn't invest felt the effects of the crash. The economy was in trouble across the country.

Before the year ended, there were more bad signs. People were buying fewer goods. They weren't putting their money in banks. Almost every business began to suffer and many companies had to let their workers go.

Some wealthy men tried to prevent panic. Multimillionaire John D. Rockefeller, Sr. tried to silence people's fears. He said that, "the fundamental conditions of the country are sound." But a lot of people were not convinced. As the 1920s ended, many feared "Coolidge Prosperity" had ended as well. ∎

Many states closed banks after the crash to prevent depositors from withdrawing all their money. Here, people besiege the Merchants Bank of Passaic, New Jersey, after it was closed by the state.

Hoover Still Confident Despite Market Crash

"**I** wish we could make him president," said Democrat Franklin D. Roosevelt. "There couldn't be a better one."

But when Roosevelt's wish came true, he wasn't happy about it. The man he had praised was Herbert Hoover. In 1928 Hoover *did* become president—but as a Republican.

It wasn't surprising that both Democrats and Republicans wanted Hoover on their tickets. His reputation was solid. He had become wealthy as a mining engineer. Then he had turned to public service. During the Great War, he led the Commission for Relief in Belgium. After the war, he headed relief efforts in Europe for President Wilson. His concern for the poor and hungry was clear.

When Hoover became president, in March 1929, business was very good. He believed it would get even better. The time was near, he said, that "poverty will be banished from this nation."

As an engineer, Hoover knew the value of careful planning. When he took office, he had a three-part plan in mind. First, he wanted new laws to help businesses and workers. He didn't think they always had to be fighting. Second, he wanted to make the government work more smoothly. Third, he wanted America to take the lead in world peace.

Hoover was careful in picking the members of his cabinet. He would need them to advise him on many matters. He remembered the bad choices Harding had made. The ten men Hoover chose were first-rate.

In the summer of 1929, the situation looked good. American business was booming. Hoover had a solid plan for the future, and top people to help him. But before he could get started, there was trouble. Well into the fall, Congress was tied up talking about tariff laws. The talks weren't all that important, but they dragged on and on.

Then, before Congress could get around to Hoover's plans, Black Thursday came. On October 24, the stock market suffered huge losses.

Many people had expected a market crash. Business had been good for many years. But could it stay good forever? On Black Thursday the country got the answer: "No!"

The show-business newspaper *Variety* told the story well. The day after the crash its headline said:

WALL STREET LAYS AN EGG

Many people had borrowed money to play the stock market. When the crash came, a lot of people lost their entire life savings.

Hoover knew the situation was serious. He tried to calm the nation. If people acted out of fear, it would make matters worse. A few weeks after the crash Hoover said, "Any lack of confidence in the economic future or the basic strength of business in the United States is foolish."

President Hoover probably believed what he said. But as 1930 approached, many Americans had their doubts. ∎

President Hoover addresses the nation in a radio broadcast from the White House.

Victims of the bloody St. Valentine's Day Massacre lay dead on the floor of a Chicago garage.

It Wasn't Hearts and Flowers

A Bloody St. Valentine's Day

On February 14, 1929, seven men stood waiting in a cold Chicago garage. It was St. Valentine's Day, but they weren't expecting a bouquet from Cupid. They were waiting for a load of stolen liquor.

As it turned out, they didn't get booze *or* bouquets. They got bullets. More than a hundred of them.

The delivery came about 10:30 that morning. A new black car with a siren stopped in front of the garage. Three men in police uniforms stepped out.

The seven men weren't worried. Their boss always paid off the police. They weren't even worried when the uniformed men started to search them. So, they didn't try to run or fight. They just did as they were told. They turned and put their hands on the back wall of the garage.

Suddenly, two men in civilian clothes appeared. They had machine guns in their hands. The men in police uniforms stepped back. And the roar of gunfire filled the air.

When it was over, all seven men were dead. The killers and the fake policemen left as quickly as they'd come. Another gangland killing had been pulled off.

The dirty work had been ordered by gangster Al Capone. He had hoped to kill Bugs Moran, another gangster. Capone and Moran both sold liquor, which was against the law. Prohibition had been in effect since 1920. But that hadn't bothered these gangsters. There was plenty of money to be made by selling bootleg liquor. That was how the gangs had grown so strong. They were willing to risk trouble with the police. Most policemen they could pay off. They were more worried about trouble with other gangsters.

Capone thought his plan was foolproof. He was sure Moran would be at the garage. And he was sure Moran wouldn't suspect the police. The trouble was, Moran never showed up that day.

And that wasn't all that went wrong for Capone. The killings became big news. The people of Chicago were really shocked this time. Since 1920, some 500 people had died in gang wars there. But this mass killing was bolder than any before.

Heroes To Some

For a long time Capone had been a celebrity. So what if he sold liquor illegally? Prohibition seemed like a joke to many people. During the 1920s, people wanted heroes and to some that's just what gangsters were. At least that's the way they seemed in the newspapers and magazines. They had plenty of money to spend. They held big parties. They visited all the expensive nightclubs.

But the bloody St. Valentine's Day Massacre was too much for most people. Capone had gone too far. After that, public opinion turned against him—and against the violent lifestyles of other gangsters as well.

■

King Tutankhamun
Ancient Egyptian Treasures Found in Tomb

The news spread around the world. It was such a shame about the boy. Dead at 18, and with such a bright future ahead of him. Still, there was no sense crying over him. After all, he'd been dead for more than 3,000 years!

His name was Tutankhamun. In his time, he had been king of Egypt. The people he ruled considered him a god. That's not how the people of the 1920s thought of him. Still, they certainly made him a celebrity.

When the kings of ancient Egypt died, their funerals were costly. Often, much of their wealth was buried with them. Thirty of those tombs were in Egypt's Valley of the Kings. They were covered over with sand so that no one would find them.

Over the centuries, though, people did find them. All of them were stripped of their riches. All except the tomb of Tutankhamun. His burial place stayed hidden for 32 centuries.

Then, in 1922, the tomb was discovered by English archaeologist Howard Carter. Carter worked for another Englishman, Lord Carnarvon. The two had been searching for Tutankhamun's tomb since 1907.

It had been a long, expensive effort. Lord Carnarvon had just about given up. He had already spent almost $500,000 on the search. But Carter felt sure they'd find the tomb. He begged Lord Carnarvon to pay for one more year's work. Lord Carnarvon agreed. But one year only.

English archaeologist Howard Carter (walking, with cane) discovered the Treasures of King Tutankhamun in 1922. They had been buried for more than 3,000 years.

The side of a lion-headed couch is packed away for shipping after being dug up in Egypt's Valley of the Kings.

Carter was sure that Tutankhamun's tomb had to lie in the Valley of the Kings. The question was, where? He had looked almost everywhere. Finally he had his men dig where ancient workers had lived. He didn't think there was much hope of finding the tomb there. But time was running out. It was the only choice he had left. Fortunately, it was the right one.

In November of 1922, Howard Carter reached the door to Tutankhamun's tomb. After more digging he came to a second door. He cut a small hole in it. Then he stuck a lit candle through it.

"Can you see anything?" Lord Carnarvon asked.

Carter could barely speak. "Yes," he said, "wonderful things. . . ."

The room was filled with golden works of art. Carter had discovered the treasures of Tutankhamun. Other rooms and more treasures were discovered. In all, more than 5,000 works of art were found. It was the richest find in the history of archaeology.

But Lord Carnarvon didn't have much time to enjoy the discovery. In April 1923, he was bitten by a mosquito. The bite became infected. Soon after, he died from it.

Carter had his problems, too. In 1923 he had a disagreement with the Egyptian government. In anger, he left Egypt and visited America. He gave many lectures and even met with President Coolidge. Because of the publicity, Tutankhamun became famous in the United States. But the name Tutankhamun was too formal for America. So the long-dead boy king became known as King Tut.

People soon were wearing King Tut hats, rings, and dresses. Broadway shows added King Tut dances to their program. Anything that even looked Egyptian became popular. Restaurants were named after him—a railroad train, too. There was even a King Tut cigar.

Finally, Carter settled his argument with the Egyptian government. He returned to Egypt to do more work in the tomb. In 1925 he found the body of Tutankhamun. It was in a nest of gold-covered coffins. It had been preserved as a mummy, wrapped in cloth.

The body was not in good shape. Still, scientists learned a little about the boy king. He was about 18 when he died. He stood about 5½ feet tall. Why he died, they couldn't say.

Some 3,200 years ago he had ruled an entire empire. He had been thought of as a god. Now, in America, he again became famous. With his name cut down to size, he helped sell cigars. ∎

The Art of the Mummy

The ancient Egyptians preserved the bodies of their dead rulers. They believed that would make the rulers happy in a life after death.

To keep the bodies from decaying, they made mummies. More than 4,600 years ago they learned to remove the body's inner organs. Those decayed quickest. Then they dried the rest of the body with special salts. The inner organs were dried separately and put in stone jars.

Two centuries later, they began covering the bodies in plaster and cloth. Some mummy makers also used melted resin from trees as protection. It kept out bacteria and dampness that could cause decay.

After being wrapped, the mummies were painted to make them look alive. Sometimes a mask of the person was put on the coffin.

Over the centuries mummy makers became very important men. They were thought of as artists and scientists. Their work lasted a long time. The mummy of Thutmosis I was found 3,500 years after his death. Thanks to the skill of the mummy makers, it was in excellent shape.

Tutankhamun's body was not so well preserved. We still have a good idea of what he looked like, though. For that we can thank the artist who made his gold mask. ∎

Thousands of New Yorkers welcomed Charles Lindbergh (hatless, in car) with a spectacular ticker-tape parade on June 13, 1927.

America's "Lone Eagle" Flies the Atlantic

It was quiet at Roosevelt Field, New York, on the morning of May 20, 1927. The sky was gray. The rain fell in an off-and-on drizzle. Most of the airplanes were tied down. They would probably stay tied down for the rest of the day. It was bad weather for flying.

But shortly before 8 o'clock, the silence was broken. An airplane engine coughed once and died. A moment later it coughed again. But this time the engine roared into action.

The plane was a silver Ryan monoplane called *The Spirit of St. Louis*. Its pilot was 25-year-old Charles Lindbergh, called "Lindy" by his friends. Despite the bad weather, Lindbergh was set to take off. A former U.S. mail pilot, he knew his plane was reliable. About 200 other planes just like it were used to fly the mail.

On this plane, though, Lindbergh had made a few changes. He had extended the wings slightly to give the plane more lift. He needed it because he was carrying an extra gas tank. The tank fit in the cabin, in front of the pilot's seat. Because it blocked his view forward, he had also added a periscope. The arrangement was awkward, but Lindbergh needed the extra gas. He was preparing to fly nonstop across the Atlantic Ocean.

No one had ever made such a flight before. A prize of $25,000 would go to the first person to do it. That wasn't the most important thing, though. Airplane pilots were a proud bunch. To them, the challenge was what mattered.

Several men had tried and failed.

Two had died in a crash. Two more had been lost at sea. Still, the promise of money and fame attracted other pilots. Some were already famous, like Navy Commander Richard Byrd, the North Pole explorer.

Charles Lindbergh was not very well known. Earlier that month, though, the newspapers had become interested in him. A few days before his attempt to fly the Atlantic, he had made a historic flight. He had flown 1,550 miles nonstop in 14 hours and 25 minutes. It was a record for time, distance, and because he had flown alone.

A "Crazy Plan"

The press was also interested because his plan was so bold. Other pilots all flew in teams. Lindbergh planned to make the flight alone. The press nicknamed him the "Lone Eagle."

Some people called his plan crazy. Clifford B. Harmon, head of an international flying club, was one of them. Such a flight would take at least a day and a half. He didn't think the young pilot could stay awake that long. And to fall asleep would mean death. "Lindbergh can't afford to risk forty winks," Harmon said. "The flight is a desperate thing. But brave!"

As Lindbergh's engine warmed up that morning, he looked to the sky. There was no break in the tent of gray. He looked at his watch. It was still a little before 8 A.M. He moved his plane into position.

Because of all the rain, the runway was soft. It was covered with pools of water. Lindbergh had to make a decision. Should he wait a day until the weather cleared? If he did, he knew he'd be taking a chance. Someone else, like Commander Byrd, might get the jump on him.

He decided he was as ready as he'd ever be. He looked at his watch again. It was 7:52 A.M. He gunned the engine and headed down the runway. Slowly, the plane picked up speed. Just at the end of the runway, he rose into the sky. For now, he was safe, on his own, and headed for France.

A Problem Staying Awake

He flew around a few storms during the day without trouble. Just before dark he flew over St. John's Harbor in Newfoundland. At that point he said goodbye to land and headed out across the Atlantic Ocean.

As he expected, Lindbergh's biggest problem was staying awake. From time to time he would slap his face. Because he was flying from west to east, the night was short. That was in his favor. In daylight it was easier to stay awake.

About 27 hours after takeoff he saw a small fishing boat. He knew he was near land. In another hour, he spotted a range of mountains. That was Ireland. He was on course!

He was about 600 miles from Paris. He was also way ahead of his schedule. Several hours later he flew over the English Channel. He had reached the mainland of Europe.

As night came on, he suddenly remembered the five sandwiches he'd brought along. He'd completely forgotten to eat! He tried to eat one, but he couldn't finish it. He was so excited he just wasn't hungry.

About an hour later, Lindbergh saw a blaze of lights below. He pointed the nose of his plane down. Below him was Le Bourget Airport in Paris, France. In 33½ hours he had flown a distance of 3,610 miles.

Because of the dark, he couldn't see the crowd of people at first. But he could hear their voices clearly. "Lindbergh! Lindbergh! Lindbergh!" they shouted. When he touched down they mobbed his plane.

After he'd stepped from the plane, Lindbergh simply said to the crowd, "My name is Charles Lindbergh."

It wasn't very much, but then action always speaks louder than words. And Lindbergh's historic solo flight had spoken volumes. ∎

A Hero's Welcome For Lindbergh

President Coolidge sent the cruiser *Memphis* to bring "Lucky Lindy" and his plane back to America. Four destroyers were waiting for the *Memphis* 100 miles out at sea. Forty airplanes and two blimps escorted the ship up Chesapeake Bay. There was a parade through the streets of Washington.

At the Washington Monument, President Coolidge was there to greet him. Lindy's mother was there too. And so was any politician who had the good luck to be invited.

The president called Lindbergh a "wholesome, earnest, fearless, courageous product of America." He praised him for his skill, saying, "The execution of his project was a perfect exhibition of his art."

Then the president awarded Lindbergh the Distinguished Flying Cross. He also made him a colonel in the Army Reserve Corps. In addition a U.S. stamp with Lindbergh's picture on it was printed. No living person had ever before been given that honor by the government.

Lindbergh spent that weekend with the president and his family. After that, he was flown to a New York airport in an army plane. From there he entered the city on a welcoming boat. More than 400 ships escorted him. All of them had their whistles and horns blasting away.

Once ashore, he was driven to city hall in an open car. All along Broadway crowds of people cheered him. Ticker tape and confetti rained down from the windows above. At city hall, Mayor Walker awarded him the State Medal of Valor.

The country went wild for Lindy. Songs were written about him. People named their children and their pets after him. A dance, the "Lindy Hop" was named after him. The Pennsylvania Railroad even named a railroad car after him.

A writer for the New York *Post* said it for everyone, "He has flown like a poem into the heart of America." He had—and America had found a hero. ∎

New York Dominates Baseball

Giants, Yankees On Top

For baseball fans in the 1920s, New York was the Promised Land. Of the ten World Series played from 1920 through 1929, eight involved New York teams.

The National League New York Giants played in four in a row. The American League New York Yankees played in a total of six. The two teams faced each other three times, the Giants winning twice, the Yankees once. Each team had many top players and colorful personalities. But on each team there was *one* man who gave his team its identity—and its greatness. ■

New York Giants "mastermind" manager John McGraw (in uniform) talks with Giants owner Charles Stoneham prior to the 1921 World Series.

John McGraw

Little Napoleon

When people talked about the Giants, they usually said "McGraw's Giants." For the Giants manager, John J. McGraw, was the soul of that team.

McGraw came to the big leagues as an infielder in 1892. He was 5-feet, 7-inches tall and weighed 155 pounds. Despite his small size, he never backed away from a fight. In 1902 he took over as manager of the Giants. Twenty years later, he was still on the job. By then he had earned the nickname "Little Napoleon."

McGraw often yelled at his players to get the most out of them. But he stood by them in a pinch. And he was quick to reward them when they played well. For many years he managed from the third base coach's box. Dressed in a Giant's uniform, he loudly encouraged his team. Just as loudly, he shouted abuse at the enemy.

In the 1920s he stepped out of uniform. Dressed in civilian clothes, he ran the team from the dugout. It made him less visible, but not less effective.

McGraw's Giants won the pennant in 1921, 1922, 1923, and 1924. No other team had even won pennants four years in a row before.

His managing was certainly made easier by the Giants many stars. He handled some of the top players of the decade. They included Casey Stengel, George Kelly, Irish Meusel, Frank Frisch, and Ross Youngs.

McGraw won his last pennant in 1924. It was clouded by trouble at the end of the season. The Giants were about to play Philadelphia. If they won, they'd win the pennant. Before the game, a Giant's player tried to bribe a Philadelphia player. He offered him $500 to "take it easy."

The player reported it, and the baseball commissioner was called in. Baseball was still hurting from the big betting scandal of the 1919 World Series. The commissioner had to act.

An investigation was started. At one point Giants stars Frisch, Kelly, and Youngs were named in the plot. Finally, they were cleared. But the player who made the offer was found guilty. He and a Giants' coach were barred forever from baseball.

The Giants had Frisch, Kelly, and Youngs for the World Series. But that still wasn't enough. They lost a tough seven game series to the Washington Senators.

The next year the Giants finished in second place behind Pittsburgh. Their string of pennants was broken. But they had set a record that would be hard to beat. No one could have expected them to win five in a row, anyway. No one that is, but John McGraw. ■

Babe Ruth

The Yankee Sultan of Swat

Babe Ruth, baseball's greatest slugger of the decade.

In 1920 the New York Yankees purchased Babe Ruth from the Boston Red Sox for $125,000. The deal sent shock waves through all of baseball. Not only was that a huge amount of money to pay for one player. But, the thought of Ruth joining what was already a pretty good batting lineup made the rest of the American League a little nervous. To say that the other teams had good reason to worry is to put it mildly.

If Babe Ruth hadn't become baseball's greatest slugger, he might just as easily have become its greatest pitcher. In five seasons as a pitcher with the Red Sox, Ruth won 87 games and lost only 45. In addition, he won three World Series games and lost none.

But the Babe had other talents as well—like hitting. As a part-time outfielder with Boston, in 1918, he hit 11 home runs to lead the league. The next year he hit 29 to lead the league again. And then in 1920, his first year as a Yankee, he hit 54! No player in either league hit as many as *20* home runs that year.

For the Yankees the timing was perfect. Until then the team had shared the Polo Grounds with the Giants. But the Giants wanted them out. They had to find a new ballpark. As it turned out, that was to the benefit of the Yankees. They were already thinking of building a new stadium. With Ruth attracting huge crowds, the time was right to move.

Two years later the team was playing in a brand-new Yankee Stadium. The Polo Ground seated only 38,000. The new park seated 65,000. And the Yankees were packing them in—thanks to the Babe. It was natural that the new park came to be called "The House That Ruth Built."

With Ruth leading them, the Yankees won six pennants in the 1920s. Three times they won the World Series. Eight times he led the league in home runs.

Promise To a Sick Boy

Ruth was bigger than life. He won the love of fans everywhere for his deeds on and off the field. He could be crude—his appetite for food and drink was huge. But he could also be gentle. His own childhood had been unhappy. As an adult, he was especially kind to young people.

Once he took an autographed baseball to a boy in a hospital. While there, he promised to hit a home run for the child, Sure enough, that afternoon he did. Later he heard that the boy had gotten better. The Babe remarked, "Best medicine in the world, a home run."

During a decade filled with many outstanding athletes, the Babe was king. His records are monuments to excellence. More than that, he has become loved and admired by his fans. As Will Rogers put it: "He's the Abraham Lincoln of baseball." ∎

World Series Heroics

In the 1920s the New York Yankees appeared in six World Series. Three times they were winners. Babe Ruth's mighty bat helped put them in all those series. And once the Yankees were there, he didn't stop swinging it. His batting average for the six series was .350. He came to bat 103 times and got 36 hits. Thirteen of them were home runs.

The 1927 season was great for both the Babe and the Yankees. He hit a record 60 home runs and batted .356. The Yankees won the pennant, and faced Pittsburgh in the World Series. New York was unstoppable, winning four games straight. The Babe came to bat 15 times and got 6 hits, 2 of them home runs. His batting average for the series was .400.

In 1928 the Yankees won the pennant again. This time their opponent in the World Series was St. Louis. Once again, they won four straight games. Amazingly, Ruth's performance was even better than the year before. He came to bat 16 times, getting 10 hits, 3 of them home runs. His average for the series was a stunning .625.

Once again he'd proved that he was truly the "Sultan of Swat."

A Football Flash Named The Galloping Ghost

Red Grange, college football's outstanding player during the 1920s.

A galloping ghost—that's how Red Grange seemed to other teams. How else could you explain what he did on the football field? He stood 5-feet, 10-inches tall and weighed 170 pounds. That's not very big for a football player. And Red wasn't very strong either. But he was the greatest football player of the 1920s. Some said maybe he was the greatest player of all time.

Red Grange played college football at the University of Illinois. In three years there, he played 20 games. In those games he ran for 3,637 yards. That's an average of more than 180 yards a game! He also scored 31 touchdowns in those 20 games.

During his career at Illinois, Grange was a hit with people both on and off the field. People admired his running and liked him because he was modest. Once he was asked to explain why he was such a good

runner. He said he couldn't. "No one ever taught me, and I can't teach anyone. If you can't explain it, how can you take credit for it?"

Whenever Grange played, the other team was always out to stop him. But that didn't make much difference. No matter how prepared they were, defensive players seemed to melt in front of him.

Take the game Illinois played against Michigan on October 19, 1924. The year before, neither team had lost a game. Many people felt this game would decide which team was the best in the country.

Before the game, the Michigan coach made a mistake. He announced that his team was prepared for Red. "Mr. Grange," he said, "will be very carefully watched." Red certainly gave them plenty to watch that day.

Grange caught the opening kick-off on his own 5 yard line. He ran straight down the middle of the field. Suddenly, he cut right, and ran past a pack of Michigan players. Then, he cut left, getting by more of them. Finally, he headed straight down field again and across the goal line. He had run 95 yards for a touchdown.

The next time Illinois got the ball, Red took off again. This time he

ran 67 yards for a touchdown. A short while later, Red handled the ball once more. What else? He ran 56 yards for a touchdown.

The Michigan players couldn't believe it. But Red was just getting started. On the next play, he ran 46 yards for his fourth touchdown. He had handled the ball only four times. He had run for 263 yards, and had scored four touchdowns. And the first half wasn't even over!

As the second half started, Red ran the ball for the fifth time. And for the fifth time, he went all the way for a touchdown. Michigan found out that there was no way to "prepare" for Red Grange.

Many people thought that the game against Michigan was Red's greatest performance. Others said it came the next year against Pennsylvania. In that game Red scored three touchdowns. He also carried the ball 36 times for 363 yards. That averaged out to better than ten yards a carry. Good enough for a first down every time he touched the ball.

That day, the Pennsylvania team learned what Michigan had the year before. When Red Grange got his hands on a football, catching him was about as easy as catching a ghost. ∎

> He had scored four touchdowns and the first half wasn't even over.

The "Flying Finn" Runs to Glory

The Olympic torch burned brightly once more in the summer of 1920. The terrible war in Europe had ended 18 months earlier. Now the world was returning to old values.

The 1916 Olympics had not been held because of the war. In 1920 the Games resumed and were held at Antwerp, Belgium. That country had suffered much during the war. It seemed a good place to rebuild the peace.

A new Olympic star was born at the 1920 Games. He burst upon the track world suddenly. But for the rest of the decade, he would dominate his sport like no athlete ever had before. His name was Paavo Nurmi and he was from Finland. They called him the "Flying Finn."

In his very first Olympic competition, Nurmi was outstanding. He won a first-place gold medal in the 10,000-meter run. He won another gold in the 10,000-meter cross-country race. He also took a second-place silver medal in the 5,000-meter race.

Nurmi didn't show any emotion when he ran. People said he looked like a mechanical man—a running machine. Newspaper writers wrote about his training secrets. Mostly, they had to guess what those secrets were. Nurmi kept to himself most of the time and didn't talk very much.

Some people thought he ate a special diet to perform so well. Once he was asked if he'd had his dried fish and black bread for the day.

"No black bread and fish *any* day," Nurmi answered. "Why should I eat things like that?"

Nurmi's real secret was hard work. Also, he planned his races carefully. When he ran, he carried a watch with him. He didn't care how fast others were running. He had figured out how fast *he* had to run to win. He felt if he just kept to the plan, he had a good chance of winning.

In the 1924 Olympics, Nurmi fared even better than in 1920. He finished first in the 1,500-meter race. The 5,000-meter race started 55 minutes later. The Flying Finn entered that too. Again he won the gold medal. He set Olympic records in both races.

Four Gold Medals

Two days later, Nurmi won the 10,000-meter cross-country race. The day after that, he entered the 3,000-meter cross-country race. He won that one, too, setting another record. The Flying Finn was the star of the 1924 Olympics. He had set *three* records and won *four* gold medals.

By the time the 1928 Olympics arrived, Nurmi was 31. He was a little past his peak. But not much. He still managed to win a gold medal for the 10,000-meter race. He also picked up second-place silver medals in two other races.

Nurmi had become a hero to the Finns and to track fans everywhere. In the 1920s he had entered ten Olympic races. He came in first in seven of them and second in the other three.

In races outside the Olympic Games, he was just as amazing. Between 1920 and 1930 he set world records in 12 different distance races. He also set a record for distance run in one hour. At the end of the hour he had gone almost 12 miles.

There was no question about it. With his medals and records Paavo Nurmi towered above all other runners of the 1920s. He had certainly earned his nickname "The Flying Finn." ∎

The 10,000-meter final of the 1928 Olympics. Paavo Nurmi (right) and fellow countryman Willie Ritola ran nearly neck and neck for 24 laps. Nurmi burst into the lead for good with only 150 yards to go.

Dempsey-Tunney Rematch Goes For "Long Count"

The big fight took place the night of September 27, 1927. More than 100,000 fans packed Soldier Field in Chicago. Most of them had one question on their minds. Could Jack Dempsey win back his title?

Dempsey had won the heavyweight championship of the world in 1919. He'd won it from 246-pound Jess Willard. In that fight, Dempsey himself only weighed 187 pounds. But he was in good shape. His punches were hard and on the mark. After three rounds of Dempsey's punches, Willard quit.

Dempsey held the title for seven years. But then he'd lost it in 1926. Now he was facing big odds. No one had ever lost the title and then won it back. But on September 27, he would get his chance. He'd be fighting Gene Tunney, who had taken Dempsey's title away the year before.

Dempsey's hopes were high. Many people thought Tunney had been lucky in the first fight. Dempsey had been out of shape. He hadn't had a fight in three years.

Dempsey was a powerful slugger. Tunney was a boxer. During that first fight Tunney moved like a dancer. He shot jabs at Dempsey that Dempsey couldn't block. They were sharp, and they stung. Dempsey kept trying to throw his knockout punch. But Tunney just wouldn't stay in one place.

It went that way for ten rounds.

Tunney danced. Dempsey swung and missed. There was no knockout. But the judges ruled in Tunney's favor. He became the new champion.

After the fight, Dempsey's face was cut and bruised. Dempsey's wife, movie star Estelle Taylor, was shocked. "How did it happen?" she asked.

"Honey," Dempsey said, "I just forgot to duck."

A Hook to the Jaw

For this second fight, Dempsey was fit. But for the first six rounds things were no different than in the first contest. Tunney danced and jabbed, danced and jabbed.

Then in the seventh round Dempsey's chance came. He caught Tunney's jaw with a left hook. Tunney was hurt. It was what Dempsey had been waiting for. He moved in, punching hard and fast. Tunney fell to the floor. Dempsey stood over him, ready to hit him if he got up.

Then the referee began shouting at Dempsey. He told the fighter he was breaking the rules. You couldn't stand over a downed opponent while the referee counted. He sent Dempsey to the other side of the ring. Only then did he begin to count.

Tunney was on his feet before the referee got to ten. His head had had time to clear. The referee had counted ten seconds. In fact, though, seventeen seconds had really passed.

For the rest of the fight Tunney continued to dance and jab. But he kept out of Dempsey's reach. Try as he might, Dempsey couldn't land another solid punch.

At the fight's end, the judges once again ruled in Tunney's favor. He was still the heavyweight champion.

Many of Dempsey's fans thought he had been cheated. But the rules were clear. You couldn't stand over your opponent while the referee was counting.

Still, one thing seemed sure. For years to come, boxing fans would argue about the "Long Count" Dempsey-Tunney fight. ■

Jack Dempsey is warned by the referee to go to a neutral corner after he knocked down Gene Tunney. The fallen champ took advantage of the referee's "long count" to rally and defeat Dempsey.

The Great George Gershwin

There are probably *some* people in America who haven't heard of George Gershwin. But it's a safe bet that even those people have heard of a number of his songs.

Such was the success and influence of George Gershwin's work during the 1920s. His songs and music seemed to be everywhere—from Broadway theaters to symphony halls, from New York City to London. Many people today regard him as America's greatest composer.

The son of Russian immigrants, George Gershwin was born in Brooklyn, New York in 1898. He began studying piano at the age of 12, and later went on to study musical composition.

In 1914 Gershwin began his career as a piano-playing song plugger for a music-publishing company. Two years later he produced his first published song.

But it wasn't until 1919 that the music world first noticed Gershwin. In that year he wrote "Swanee." The song became an instant smash hit when it was performed by the popular entertainer, Al Jolson, in the show *Sinbad.*

Gershwin reached his greatest fame as a Broadway composer. During the 1920s he composed the music for one hit musical after another. These shows included *Lady, Be Good* (1924), *Tip Toes* (1925), *Oh, Kay* (1926), *Strike Up the Band* (1927), *Funny Face* (1927), and most recently *Girl Crazy* (1930).

While George wrote the music for these popular shows, his brother Ira wrote the song lyrics. Together they've produced some of the most popular tunes in American music. "Fascinating Rhythm," "Oh, Lady Be Good," "Embraceable You," "I Got Rhythm," "'S' Wonderful," and "Someone to Watch Over Me," are just a few examples of their many hits.

But George Gershwin's musical reputation is based on more than his work as a Broadway composer. He has also written many lengthy classical and jazz compositions. Among them are *Concerto in F* (1925), *An American in Paris* (1928), and his most famous piece, *Rhapsody in Blue* (1924).

Gershwin wrote *Rhapsody in Blue* specifically at the request of the famous jazz orchestra leader, Paul Whiteman. It had its premiere at a concert in New York City on February 12, 1924. Gershwin himself performed the work on piano along with Whiteman's orchestra.

The composition was immediately hailed as a masterpiece of American music. Since its debut, only six years ago, it has been performed hundreds of times by solo pianists, jazz bands, classical orchestras, choral groups, and tap and ballet dancers. And *Rhapsody in Blue* raised Gershwin's reputation far above that of a "popular song" composer. He's now considered one of America's greatest "serious" composers as well.

As the decade ended, George Gershwin's fame and success continued to increase. As an accomplished pianist and versatile composer, George Gershwin has no equal anywhere on the American music scene. ■

Composer and pianist George Gershwin.

A 'Lost Generation' of Writers

The Great War had proved to be a powerful killer. Along with the millions of dead men, ideals seemed to die as well.

For some people there seemed to be little purpose in life after the war. Why worry about the future? What good had that done the boys who went off to fight?

Ideas of truth and justice didn't seem worth much anymore. As the 1920s began, there were new ideas in the air. Live for the day! Get it while you can!

Many American authors felt out of place. American audiences didn't seem very interested in reading books anymore. They were only interested in what money could buy.

Willa Cather, Theodore Dreiser, and John Dos Passos wrote novels about that. They took a hard look at the world of business. To them, most businessmen were shallow, selfish people.

Sinclair Lewis also wrote about Americans who led empty lives. He described them in *Main Street* and other best-selling books. His novel *Babbitt* was about George Babbitt, just such a man. Before long, the name became part of a language. A "Babbitt" was someone interested only in money and material things.

Some writers found a solution in travel. Ernest Hemingway decided to get away from America. He had seen Europe during the war. He felt Europeans cared more about the finer things in life. That was the place for a writer.

Gertrude Stein, an older American writer in Paris, became friends with Hemingway. She took an interest in him and helped him with his writing. She often helped the young

Americans who drifted around Europe after the war. She called them "a lost generation."

Hemingway used those words at the beginning of his first novel. It was called *The Sun Also Rises*. It gave a picture of how his generation lived. It became a best seller. Other "expatriates," as they were called, were the poets Ezra Pound and T. S. Eliot. They often wrote about the meaninglessness of American life.

F. Scott Fitzgerald was another member of Hemingway's lost generation. His first novel, *This Side of Paradise*, published in 1920, was a great success. It also shocked many Americans. It told about changes in morals that were taking place. Before

the war, young people were supposed to be serious and proper. As Fitzgerald told it, that was old-fashioned. Young people were living for today. Tomorrow could take care of itself. Dancing and drinking were a way of life. Even nice girls went to all-night parties. The "Roaring Twenties" were underway!

Fitzgerald wrote other popular books during the decade, including *Flappers and Philosophers* (1920), *Tales of the Jazz Age* (1922), and *The Great Gatsby* (1925).

After that, Fitzgerald's writing took a back seat to his partying. The "Jazz Age" was in full swing. Like the characters in his books, he decided to join them. ∎

F. Scott Fitzgerald, one of the most popular writers of the 1920s.

Crowds gather outside a theater in New York to see the first talking motion picture, *The Jazz Singer*.

The Movies Talk

The actor on the screen finished playing the piano. Then he looked out toward the movie audience and spoke.

"Wait a minute! Wait a minute!" he said. "You ain't heard nothin' yet!" How right he was.

The actor's name was Al Jolson. The movie was *The Jazz Singer*. The date was October 6, 1927. It was a historic turning point in the movie business. For the first time in a major movie, the public heard voices as well as music.

There had already been a few movies with music. Most movies, though, were silent. Sometimes when the actors spoke, the words were written on the screen. At other times, the audience had to guess what they were saying. Many people thought that was the best way. They thought movies should be seen but not heard.

Even Al Jolson was not happy about sound coming to movies. He made a lot of money doing stage shows. He was worried that "talkies" would take away business from live acts. Finally, though, he agreed to be in *The Jazz Singer*. The movie was a big success. Soon, almost all movies were "talkies."

For actors and actresses with good voices, talkies were fine. For others, they meant ruin. John Gilbert was a romantic star of silent movies. He looked handsome and strong. His voice, though, was very high. When he spoke in his first "talkie," the audience roared with laughter. After that his career fell apart.

Some people still like the silent movies better. The writer Ernest Betts wrote: "There is something monstrous about a speaking film."

Most people thought differently. Because of "talkies," more and more people started going to the movies. In 1927 American movie attendance was about 60,000,000 a week. By 1929 it was about 110,000,000 a week. It looked like the talkies were here to stay. ■

Charles Lindbergh
Hero of the Skies

The 1920s saw more than its share of heroes. Some won fame by digging up mummies. Some made their names by swatting baseballs or running with footballs. Others thrilled movie viewers—or made them roar with laughter. One hero just sat still—although his perch was on a flagpole.

It made no difference whether these heroes were serious or silly. The world was recovering from the most horrible war in history. Heroes of any kind were welcome.

Most welcome of all was a shy young fellow from America's mid-

Charles Lindbergh and his wife, Anne Morrow.

west. There was nothing flashy about him. He would be out of place in a speakeasy. An all-night party held no interest for him. The name on his pilot's license was Charles A. Lindbergh. The newspapers called him "The Lone Eagle." To most people, he was just Lindy.

At age 26 he had flown the Atlantic, nonstop—alone. He had set a record. There was a prize. There were many awards and honors. There were many parades. But there was much more to his triumph than all that.

Lindbergh's accomplishment was not just for himself or his country. It was a victory for the human spirit. Lindy had proved that courage and hard work counted. There *were* values to be prized. The decent, daring young man had sparked a flame of hope in a weary world.

An Active Youth

As a child, Lindy had spent summers on a farm in Minnesota. He loved the outdoors. He also loved machines. He was a responsible boy. At age 6 he had his own .22 rifle. At 11, his father taught him to drive a Model T Ford. At 14, he could take an automobile engine apart and repair it.

Lindbergh went on to study engineering for two years at the University of Wisconsin. But his real interest was flying. In 1922 he switched to an aviation school. From that time forward airplanes were at the center of his life. He flew stunt planes for a while. Then he earned his wings flying with the Army Reserve in Texas.

In 1925 he began flying the United States mail. The flights were often made in rough weather. It gave him good experience. During a more peaceful flight, an idea came to him. He had been flying long distances in his work. Why couldn't he fly across the Atlantic? He decided that he could—if he had the right plane.

In February 1927 he got that plane. It was a silver, single-engine Ryan monoplane. He named it *Spirit of St. Louis*. Three months later, he and his plane made history.

The Ambassador's Daughter

After the celebration, Lindy didn't waste time. He made public appearances around the country. He wasn't promoting himself. He was promoting aviation.

In December 1927 Lindbergh flew to Mexico City. There, he stayed at the home of the ambassador to Mexico. And there, he met the ambassador's daughter, Anne Morrow. She was beautiful and intelligent. They liked each other from the start.

Reporters often wanted to know about Lindy's private life. For them he had a standard answer: "What's that got to do with aviation?" But there was no hiding his love for Anne. In May of 1929 they were married.

As the decade ended, Lindy remained a hero around the world. He helped put aviation in the public's eye. He was an officer in a new airline company. And his lovely bride was expecting a child.

His flight forecast seemed to be: "Clear skies ahead!" ∎

Lady with a Mission

Nancy Astor

Nancy Astor never had to worry about money. When she was born in 1879, her family could only afford a small house. By the time she was six, though, they were well off.

She grew up in a big house in Richmond, Virginia. When she was 11, her family bought a second house in the country. Nancy loved to spend time there. She often went fishing in the nearby streams. And most of all, she loved to ride horses.

In 1908 Nancy moved to England and married Waldorf Astor. He was a very rich man. She could have lived a life of ease. But that wasn't to her taste. She was smart, tough, and full of energy. She had to keep busy. And she had to help others.

Because of that, she became involved in politics. Her husband served in England's Parliament. He represented a district in Plymouth in the House of Commons. Nancy worked closely with him as his assistant. With that experience, she got to know the people of Plymouth well. And she came to understand their problems.

She didn't just sit behind a desk. She spent part of her time helping the poor. Often she visited the sick in hospitals. When the Great War came, Nancy became even more active. She had a Red Cross hospital built on her property. She spent much time working there.

A Challenge in Parliament

After the war, her husband became Viscount Astor. As a nobleman, he could no longer serve in the House of Commons. But Nancy could. A new law stated that for the first time, women would be allowed to serve in Parliament.

Nancy thought about it. It would be a challenge. She certainly understood what needed to be done in Plymouth. She had the brains and the energy for the job. And it would be worth trying—just to see if she could! She decided to go ahead with it.

In 1919 Nancy ran for the office her husband had held. She worked hard and made many speeches. The people in Plymouth already knew about her hospital work. Although she was rich, she had won the respect of the common people.

When the votes were counted, she had won by a large majority. She became the first woman ever to serve in the House of Commons.

From the beginning she was interested in equal opportunity for women. In 1920 she helped women get jobs with the police. She also worked to make inheritance laws fairer to women. She also maintained her concern for the poor. And she took special interest in children. She helped pass many laws protecting their rights.

Besides her political work, she was a great hostess. Rich and famous people from around the world visited her home at Cliveden. George Bernard Shaw, the writer, was an especially welcome guest.

But the rich and famous were not her chief concern. Women, children, and the poor looked to Lady Astor to represent their interests. As the 1920s ended, she remained a powerful symbol of strength for all of them. ∎

Lady Nancy Astor, first woman to be elected to Great Britain's Parliament.

India's "Great Soul"
Mohandas Gandhi

The British were worried. For many years they had ruled India. They had taken a great deal of wealth from the Asian country. Now the Indian people were demanding freedom.

The Indians had revolted before. But the British Army had managed to stop them. The British guns were powerful. Now, though, they were facing an enemy that guns couldn't stop.

He was an Indian named Mohandas Gandhi. He had given the British one year to free his country. He had warned that if they didn't, he would use his weapon against them. It was even more powerful than the British guns. His weapon was nonviolence, and it had the power of truth behind it. For years he had been learning how to use that power.

Born in 1869, Gandhi grew up in a well-to-do Indian family. His childhood was pleasant. His middle-class parents taught him how to be honest and fair. As he grew to manhood, he always remembered one event of his youth. Foolishly, he had stolen some gold from his brother. Finally, he felt so guilty he had to tell his father. He feared his father would be very angry at him. Instead, his father began to cry. It moved Gandhi more than if his father had hit him. He later said the tears of his father had cleansed his heart. That event showed him how powerful nonviolence could be.

In his late teens he studied law in England. At 24 he went to South Africa to be a law clerk. Because he was from Asia, the whites in South Africa treated Gandhi unfairly. He began to work to get just treatment for his people. It was then he began to use the power of *Satyagraha*—an Indian word for "truth force."

In 1913 the South African government passed a series of laws that took away many freedoms from Indians who lived there. Gandhi led thousands of people in opposing the laws. This was called civil disobedience—*satyagraha* in action. Gandhi made it clear they would not use violence. "We will overcome our enemies with love, not with hate or violence. We will convert them from wrong-doing to right-doing."

The struggle lasted for years. Many of Gandhi's followers were killed. Many were jailed, as was Gandhi himself. Finally, the government gave the Indians some of their freedoms back.

Gandhi returned to India in 1915. There he began to help Indians get more freedom from the British. In 1919 he tried to use *satyagraha* to change an unfair law. He told his people to close their businesses. That started more trouble. People began to demonstrate. On April 13, government troops fired at an unarmed crowd. Hundreds of Indians were killed and thousands were wounded.

A Term in Prison

Gandhi saw that his people were not yet ready for *satyagraha*. He would have to teach them its meaning. Also, he saw that the British must leave India. Only then could his country be free. So, in 1920, he wrote a new constitution for the Indian National Congress.

In 1922 he was arrested for writing articles against British rule. He admitted it was true. But he said it was his duty not to cooperate with evil. He was sentenced to six years in prison. But because of bad health, he only served two.

When he got out, people were calling him *Mahatma*. That meant "Great Soul." He was loved my millions. He had taught them about their rights. He had showed them the power of nonviolence. Now he went all over India teaching his ideas.

At the end of 1928 the Indian Congress made a demand. They wanted more freedom from the British. If they didn't get it in a year, they would fight for complete independence. Their fight would be nonviolent. It would be led by Gandhi.

On December 31, 1929, the British still hadn't given in. Now they would have to face a powerful force—*satyagraha*. And they would have to deal with Gandhi, the "Great Soul." It was no wonder they were worried. ∎

Mohandas Gandhi has led a decade-long struggle for India's independence.

Leon Trotsky went from war hero to exile in the space of ten short years.

A Fallen Hero

Leon Trotsky

Leon Trotsky was a Soviet hero in 1921. He had taken a ragtag bunch of men and turned them into the Red Army. And with that army he had crushed the forces that opposed the Revolution.

But as the 1920s ended, he found himself out of power. Scorned by his former comrades, he was forced to live abroad. In ten years, he had gone from hero to outcast.

Leon Trotsky was born Lev Davidovitch Bronstein in 1879 in Yanovka, Russia. His father was a Jewish farmer. At 17 the young man went to the Baltic port of Nikolayev. There he became interested in socialism. Soon he became a Marxist and a revolutionary. He was arrested several times for union activities. He often spoke out against the tsar, Russia's ruler. As punishment, in 1900 he was sent to live in Siberia, an area far from Moscow. It was very cold and empty there. But that didn't stop him. His writings were sneaked out of Siberia and read by revolutionaries. Because of them, he earned the nickname "The Pen."

In 1902 he escaped from Siberia and left Russia. He visited Belgium, France, Germany, and England. Every place he went, he continued to promote revolution. In London, he helped Vladimir Lenin with *Spark*, a revolutionary newspaper.

During that time, there were two main revolutionary groups in Russia. They didn't always agree. The Bolsheviks thought the revolutionary party should be very tightly organized. The Mensheviks favored a looser structure. Lenin took the Bolshevik side. Trotsky went with the Mensheviks. His position, though, was somewhere between the two.

Trotsky returned to Russia in 1905. He was exiled to Siberia once again after he continued to engage in revolutionary activity. He returned to Russia for good in 1917, after the March revolution that toppled the tsar from power. This time Trotsky teamed up with Lenin. He joined the Bolshevik Party as Lenin's assistant.

Once the Bolsheviks took power in November 1917, Trotsky became one of its leaders. In 1918 the Bolsheviks were forced into a civil war. And Trotsky led the fight against the White Army, the tsar's supporters. He started with a few thousand Bolsheviks, the Red Guard. By 1920 he had built it into the powerful Red Army, with a force of five million soldiers.

By November 1920 the last resistance in the civil war was over. In 1921 Trotsky was at the height of his popularity. That year he sent troops to stop a revolt at Kronstadt. Thousands of men were killed by the Red Army. Because of the deaths, his popularity started to lessen. At the same time, a man named Josef Stalin was rising fast. Lenin had been thinking of getting rid of Stalin. But then Lenin suffered a stroke. Stalin moved ahead, putting his supporters in important jobs.

Trotsky the Intellectual

When Lenin died in 1924, Trotsky and Stalin fought for power. They each had different ideas about how power should be used. Trotsky was interested in spreading world revolution. Stalin's interest lay inside Russia. "Socialism in one country" was his slogan.

Trotsky was an intellectual. He was more of a thinker than Stalin. The practical Stalin used that to his advantage. He said the country needed a man who got things done. It didn't need someone who was all theory.

Bit by bit, Trotsky was pushed away from power. In 1924 the Central Committee of the Communist party censured Trotsky. After finding fault with him, they fired him as commissar for war. In 1925 he was forbidden to make speeches. In 1927 he was kicked out of the Communist party, and early in 1928 he was sent to Siberia. It was the third time in his life he was imprisoned there. This time though, it wasn't the tsar who sent him. It was his former comrades.

He continued to write articles attacking Stalin. Of course, they were sneaked out of Siberia. But finally, in 1929, he was kicked out of the Soviet Union.

Leon Trotsky—revolutionary and Civil War hero—was an exile. He could no longer live in the nation he helped create. ∎

OUR CENTURY: 1920-1930

GLOSSARY

ACLU: the American Civil Liberties Union, a group concerned with ensuring people's freedom of speech.

Black Thursday: the day the U.S. stock market "crashed" on October 24, 1929, triggering the Great Depression.

Bolsheviks: the Russians who successfully overthrew the Russian monarch, the Tsar, in 1917.

the Charleston: a popular dance craze during the 1920s.

civil war: a war between different groups of people within the same country.

court-martial: a procedure for trying someone within the military service.

depression: an economic period in which there is very high unemployment and a financial crisis that makes it hard to create jobs.

fascism: a government system in which a strong leader is allowed to rule regardless of whether he or she has the people's support. Fascist governments do not allow any opposition groups.

flappers: a term used to refer to women who wore certain modern hair and clothing styles during the 1920s.

Il Duce: an Italian word meaning "leader and dictator" used to refer to Benito Mussolini.

immigrant: a person who leaves his or her native land to start a new life in another.

mummy: a body that has been preserved after death by removing the inner organs and taking other measures to prevent decay.

Prohibition: a period in the United States when Americans were legally prevented from making or selling alcoholic beverages.

quota: a legal limit set for the number of people allowed to do something. During the 1920s, there were quotas set for the number of people allowed to immigrate to the United States from other countries.

Reds: a slang expression for Communists.

talkies: movies in which sound accompanied the images. The first talkie was Al Jolson's *The Jazz Singer* in 1927.

theory of evolution: the scientific theory, based on biological research, that human beings evolved from other mammals such as apes.

wireless: an older term for what we now call a radio.

BOOKS FOR FURTHER READING

The titles listed below provide more detailed information about some of the people and events described in this book. Ask for them at your local library or bookstore.

The Crash of 1929. Biel (Lucent Books)

Herbert C. Hoover: 31st President of the United States. Polikaf (Garrett Ed. Corp.)

John D. Rockefeller. Shuker (Silver Burdett)

Lottie, Daughter of the Depression. Reasonover (Winston-Derek)

Magic in the Dark: A Young Viewers History of the Movies. Meyer (Facts on File)

The Story of the Great Depression. Stein (Childrens Press)

PLACES TO WRITE OR VISIT

Museum of the Cinema
360 McGill Street
Montreal, Quebec H2Y 2E9

Museum of Television and Radio
25 West 52nd Street
New York, New York 10019

The Smithsonian Institution
1000 Jefferson Drive S.W.
Washington, D.C. 20560

INDEX